W9-AOP-366

BRIAN HAGGARD

Crazy-Quilted
MEMORIES

BEAUTIFUL EMBROIDERY BRINGS YOUR FAMILY PORTRAITS TO LIFE

C&T PUBLISHING

Text copyright © 2011 by Brian Haggard

How-to photography copyright © 2011 by Brian Haggard and Kevin Head

Quilt photography and artwork copyright © 2011 by C&T Publishing, Inc.

Publisher: *Amy Marson*

Creative Director: *Gailen Runge*

Acquisitions Editor: *Susanne Woods*

Editor: *Liz Aneloski*

Technical Editors: *Ann Haley and Gailen Runge*

Copyeditor/Proofreader: *Wordfirm Inc.*

Cover Designer: *Kristen Yenche*

Book Designer: *Rose Sheifer-Wright*

Production Coordinator: *Jenny Leicester*

Production Editor: *Julia Cianci*

Illustrator: *Wendy Mathson*

Quilt photography by *Christina Carty-Francis and Diane Pedersen* of C&T Publishing, Inc., unless otherwise noted

All rights reserved. No part of this work covered by the copyright hereon may be used in any form or reproduced by any means—graphic, electronic, or mechanical, including photocopying, recording, taping, or information storage and retrieval systems—without written permission from the publisher. The copyrights on individual artworks are retained by the artists as noted in *Crazy-Quilted Memories*. These designs may be used to make items only for personal use or donation to nonprofit groups for sale. Each piece of finished merchandise for sale must carry a conspicuous label with the following information: Designs copyright © 2011 by Brian Haggard from the book *Crazy-Quilted Memories* from C&T Publishing, Inc.

Attention Copy Shops: Please note the following exception—publisher and author give permission to photocopy pages 49 and 86–94 for personal use only.

Attention Teachers: C&T Publishing, Inc., encourages you to use this book as a text for teaching. Contact us at 800-284-1114 or www.ctpub.com for lesson plans and information about the C&T Creative Troupe.

We take great care to ensure that the information included in our products is accurate and presented in good faith, but no warranty is provided nor are results guaranteed. Having no control over the choices of materials or procedures used, neither the author nor C&T Publishing, Inc., shall have any liability to any person or entity with respect to any loss or damage caused directly or indirectly by the information contained in this book. For your convenience, we post an up-to-date listing of corrections on our website (www.ctpub.com). If a correction is not already noted, please contact our customer service department at ctinfo@ctpub.com or at P.O. Box 1456, Lafayette, CA 94549.

Trademark (™) and registered trademark (®) names are used throughout this book. Rather than use the symbols with every occurrence of a trademark or registered trademark name, we are using the names only in the editorial fashion and to the benefit of the owner, with no intention of infringement.

Library of Congress Cataloging-in-Publication Data

Haggard, Brian.

Crazy-quilted memories : beautiful embroidery brings your family portraits to life / Brian Haggard.

   p. cm.

ISBN 978-1-60705-227-2 (soft cover)

1. Quilting--Patterns. 2. Embroidery. I. Title.

TT835.II254 2011

746.46--dc22

                    2010043694

Printed in China

10 9 8 7 6 5 4 3 2 1

Contents

Dedication

To all the quilt artists who have been stifled by
rules, measurements, exact ¼" seam allowances,
and perfectly spaced quilting stitches.
May this book set you free!

Acknowledgments

Thanking everyone who had a part in making this book a reality is impossible, so let me start by saying thanks to everyone who ever said, "You should write a book." To each of my art teachers through the years who taught me that life can be fulfilling in spite of the "3 R's," I am forever indebted. I must say that I would not have written this at all if it hadn't been for the instruction, encouragement, and love of my grandmother, Juanita Taylor. Her spirit was with me every step of the way. Next is the gratitude that I feel every day to my parents, Rich and Deb Haggard, for being my number one fans. They have always been, and always will be, appreciative of my artistic endeavors. My thanks to my aunt, Darlene Byers, for sharing her stash of family photos and helping complete the picture of my father's heritage. Suzy Kaster is my surrogate mother and a great friend who's been there from the beginning with constant encouragement. To my brother, Shane, and my sister-in-law, Shelly Haggard—I'm grateful for their continued encouragement, as well as their work in getting the proposal for this book under way. I love Shane's story that begins this book; it exactly paints the picture in my mind that I'm trying to convey with this work. I've been through thick, thin, and a lot of thread with my lifelong friends, Colleen Anderson and Chris Opsahl. They inspire me to do many things, with this work being just one. I'm thankful to my partner, Kevin Head, for his confidence that we'd always get everything done on time and for his help in making it happen. To Jane Haganman and Alissa Thompson, for always providing the kick in the pants to keep me going, for their unwavering friendship, and for being the voices not only in my head but also in my ear—thank you. I'm grateful to Linda Hale, Teri Dougherty, and all the great women at The Back Door Quilts for their advice and support. Melissa Taylor taught me the quilting rules (which I now gleefully ignore) and added her artistry to my work with her beautiful quilting. My work is better for knowing her. To Janet Brandt, for her constant encouragement and support and for teaching me how to navigate the uncharted territory of publishing, I give my heartfelt thanks. And Sandy Elliott—her retirement from a career of technical writing couldn't have come at a better time. Sandy volunteered to get my ideas onto paper. Without her patience and hard work, you wouldn't be reading this now. Thank you, Sandy, for always being that constant voice saying "yes, you can" and "you were meant to do this."

Preface

A Story of Creative Inspiration from the Imagination of My Brother, Shane Haggard

My ancestral home holds so many memories; it has been a part of my family's legacy for more than a century. It now belongs to me. I vowed to restore this vintage lady to her former grandeur. I decided to begin my journey in the stagnant attic, felted in dust and layers of cobwebs. Making my way to the attic staircase, I found a door, wider than normal, allowing for larger furniture. I became captivated by how ornate the staircase was, with its lovely smooth patina, almost forgetting my original mission. Ascending the stairs and pushing open the meticulously carved door, I was quickly catapulted back to another time.

The dark, smelly, creepy attic ran the entire length of the house. Days passed as I worked at the daunting task of cleaning and organizing my treasure. Frequently, precious finds from Great-Grandma's haberdashery were unearthed. Stories of the haberdashery had been passed down, but how much was truth and how much had been embellished? This had always been a mystery, until now.

Buried in a wooden box were several old photographs of her store. The finest millinery items and Great-Grandma with her army of seamstresses adorned many of the pictures. Studying the pictures, I realized that several of the fixtures that had once adorned the walls of the haberdashery now surrounded me. I was standing at the beginning of the story. The cleaning and clearing had finally come to a head, and every minute spent on this project was paying off; I had finally made my way to the storage units.

Glass containers were filled with buttons—wood, shell, metal, and bone—from all over the world. I found sewing implements, including a sewing bird (page 64) that was a little worn and covered in cobwebs and dust. Hundreds of pairs of scissors and thousands of straight pins and sewing needles filled the drawers. Scissors from far-off places had adornments molded in the handles and were still sharp and stunningly graceful. The patina of age graced the crevices between the filigrees and floral images. The pincushions were ornate and truly works of art—patches of velvet and satin pieced together with intricate stitches in a variety of patterns, trimmed in faded and aging lace. Some were leaking sawdust like open wounds. The cupboards brimmed with velvet, cotton, satin, and silk fabrics. The room was filled with the smell of mothballs and just a slight undertone of lavender. I remember my grandmother always using lavender water to keep insects away.

My grandmother (daughter to my great-grandmother) is the reason I am so fond of all things creative. It was she who taught me to sew and to embellish using nothing more than a vision and the art of manipulating a needle.

Months passed as I debated how to honor my ancestors using this grand treasure. I finally determined that the greatest honor would be to create one-of-a-kind treasures to bind the fibers of time. This book before you is the result of many years and many hours creating such labors of love. While honoring my great-grandmother's memory, I have also honored the family, before and after her, by using photographs on fabric in many of the pieces. It is important to honor those who pass the creative spirit to each of us. Find your creative spirit and, using your own treasured findings, begin to tell your stories.

Introduction

Creativity is never born out of fear.

This book is something new! As you read, you will find that it is not like traditional quilt books. The heart of what I want to show you is how to start with something you really love and let it build from there. Measurements don't matter. Design as you go—let the piece grow organically and let your imagination take you where it will. You won't get bored because the design becomes a work of the heart. When I make a piece, the design happens as I work on it; I don't know where it will go when I start. I enjoy the type of quilting that I do because it's not predictable.

Choosing Fabrics

Fabric moves me, and I only purchase what I love.

First and foremost, as an artist, you must always select fabric that you love; choose textures, colors, and styles that inspire you. Find pieces that create an illusion or jog a memory—whether it's from childhood or the present day, it should mean something to you. These fabrics will form the base of your quilt. Working with your personal palette of colors, textures, and types will give you that wonderful sense of home and history.

I like working in a neutral palette. I don't like a lot of busyness. I want my stitching, not the pattern of the fabric, to become the artwork.

Don't be chintzy with fabric. Buy the best you can find. You want a wonderful piece of art today and in 100 years—remember, you are the creator of the next generation of art. I often use 100% cotton because I like the feel of an all-natural fabric. Consider upholstery-weight cotton fabric. I love it! I use it in edges, borders, and so on, because I like the weight of it. Once in a while, when I long for the sheen of silk or satin or the comforting weave of linen, I go for it!

I showcase my handwork on nonbusy fabrics. When choosing fabrics for your quilt, don't let bold colors and patterns overpower the beauty you'll create with your embellishments. Embellishments tend to get lost in powerfully patterned fabrics.

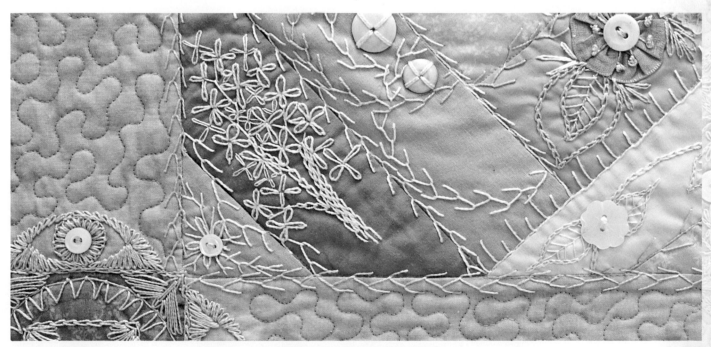

Handwork showcased on nonbusy fabrics.

Creating a Look

My look is vintage and timeworn and suggests a tattered past. I achieve it by using things that have a history, created by the choices I have made. I create the vintage look by picking, dyeing, pressing, and heating fabrics and trims.

What do you have? Pull out your stash and find what you love! Look around for things that inspire you and put them together. Find a beautiful vintage fabric that speaks to you and buy a couple of yards for borders, backing, and binding. This is how I design, and it's what I want to teach you. Relax and let the art take you where it wants to go.

Choosing Fabrics

Start by choosing natural fabrics with an aged, worn feeling. Press with a very hot iron. If you use steam, the fabric will flatten and compress as if it's been lying in a drawer for years. If you use spray starch, you'll get a polished sheen; the threads will be mashed by the heat of the iron under the starch and will blend into the fabrics, giving them the appearance of having been laundered many times. All-natural fabrics and all-natural threads won't melt with a hot iron like synthetics will. (You can use synthetics, but you'll need to put a pressing cloth over them, so they won't stick to the face of your iron. That, my friends, is not pretty!)

To create your personal look, start with a favorite fabric and use it as your main focus. Then start auditioning other fabrics. It's an audition process—if a fabric isn't working, don't be afraid to take it out or put another one in until you achieve the balance you want.

In *Love Letters* (page 56), the brown floral was the main focus, setting a framework for all the intricate stitching. Sometimes the fabric can be the quilt's main focus, while other times it will be merely the background. Never be afraid of being bold or outrageous. Sometimes that's what it takes to find the inner artist.

Detail of *Love Letters* (full quilt, page 56)

After the quilt top is finished, audition the border fabrics. In the photo below, the darker inner-border fabric creates a frame around the blocks, whereas the lighter outer-border fabric helps outline and show off the handwork in the blocks.

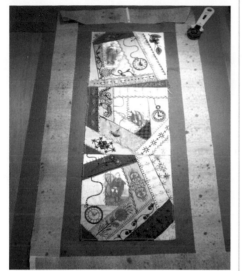

Auditioning border fabrics.

Choosing a Color Palette

The color palette you choose creates a mood, an ambience, whether you are using completely new materials or vintage pieces. If you want a new look, use newer, brighter fabrics. If you prefer an older, vintage look, choose colors that have an older appeal to them.

In *A Silken Tribute* (page 70), all the fabrics were brand-new 100% silk. However, the inspiration was to make an old handed-down fragment of life. All of the beads, buttons, and charms were brand new but were chosen to have that old, weathered look, so everything would be cohesive. The felt flower and leaf appliqués were made out of new felt and thread, and the new silk ribbon was a brighter blue than I wanted, so I used Brian's Aging Mist (page 95) to make it all look very old and weathered.

Detail of *A Silken Tribute* (full quilt, page 70)

Creating the Aged Look

Create fabric with an aged appeal that blends with the overall timeworn look of what is actually a brand-new quilt.

Pieces for the quilts can be aged before or after they are added to the quilt. Aging pieces before adding them to the quilt creates a clean dividing line between pieces, while aging them afterward gives a softer, more blended look.

You'll need two spray bottles, one filled with water and the other with Brian's Aging Mist (page 95).

1. Thoroughly dampen the strips of fabric with the water spray.

2. Spatter and mist the fabric with Brian's Aging Mist. The mist will immediately bleed into the dampened fabric.

3. Iron the fabric to heat set the mist in place.

Borders after aging.

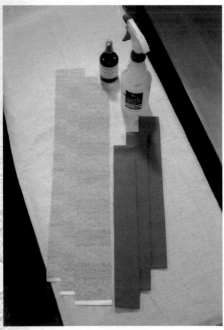

Borders before aging.

Note

You can use a similar aging technique for organza, a synthetic fabric. Gather the fabric to make a flower and tie it off. Spray it with water and, using a pressing cloth, squash it under the iron, making it look tired. Place it on a piece of paper and spray it with Brian's Aging Mist. Iron the still-wet fabric using an old pressing cloth. (Some dye residue will come off on the pressing cloth, so don't use your best linens.) The fabric is magically aged and ready to appliqué to your project.

Adding the History

Selecting, Scanning, and Printing Photographs on Fabric

Note

No antique photos were harmed in the making of these quilts.

Cotton twill PhotoFabric (CTPF), from Crafter's Images, is my favorite brand of photo-transfer fabric. It's available on a roll and has a paper backing so it can be used in an inkjet printer. As you need it, cut it into 8½″ × 11″ pieces for use in your printer.

Tip

Do not cut the Cotton Twill Photo Fabric off the roll before you're ready to use it. When it's cut and lies around too long, it flattens out and doesn't go through the printer as well. It should have a little curl, like it does when it comes off the roll.

Photo-editing software (e.g., Adobe Photoshop, Picasa) allows you to manipulate photos of different quality and coloring or from different times into a uniform style.

In this example, one of the original photos (in the bottom left corner of this shot) was quite faded. However, notice how well it printed on the photo-transfer fabric after it was scanned into the computer and edited with simple photo-editing software.

Original photos and digitally enhanced photos printed on CTPF.

1. Scan the photographs into your computer and edit them using photo-editing software.

2. Print the photos onto the CTPF. Print multiple photos onto one sheet to avoid wasting any of the CTPF.

3. Cut apart the individual photos while the paper backing is still on the CTPF.

4. Peel the paper backing from the fabric and flatten the photos on your cutting board. Use a straight-edge and a rotary cutter to trim each photo (make sure to leave at least ¼″ around the subject in the photo to allow for the seam when sewing it to the next piece of fabric).

Manipulating Photographs

A good example of photograph manipulation can be seen on *Button, Button, Who's Got the Button?* (page 63). The center of each block has a focal point of a larger image made from my antique sewing implements collection. While working in my studio, I got the idea to create fabric from found objects lying around. This inspiration came to me from my love of buttons. I started by placing one of my sewing implements in the center of the scanner and surrounding it with buttons turned upside down to fill in around it.

Tip

You may not always like your first image. Don't be afraid to audition different items on the scanner face and preview them through the scanner eye to determine whether the balance and harmony are how you want them. If not, move things around and try again. It took me a couple of tries to figure out how I wanted the buttons to look. At first, I tried the scanner's white background, but it didn't have the look I wanted. I discovered that choosing a color that's in the fabric of the quilt (mine was black) makes the items pop!

I was concerned that my quilt would get boring with all the images cut from the same piece of fabric, so I scaled the images up and down in the photo-editing software to add variety. Nothing was wasted, because whatever I cut away from the photo pictures for the center of the blocks, I used for foundation piecing. The teeny-tiny button print that looks like calico is actually the same image repeated 30 times on one page, which makes it look like an original calico print!

In one of the classes I taught, a student brought her mother's wedding certificate, wedding bands, and a love letter to her mother from her father. We created fabric from her personal items to cut up and put in the quilt. We used some cream silk from her mother's wedding dress to back the items on the scanner. Since part of her mother's wedding dress was used in the quilt, everything was cohesive. This is a great way to make a quilt not only personal but also an archive of family memorabilia.

The Legacy, the Lineage— Labeling Your Art

Labeling is very important to the history and legacy of your art. It will keep the dream alive long after you are gone. I've always been fascinated by quilt dating and documentation. Seeing how people have left their mark makes me want to preserve the history of my art for long after my life has ended. There are many ways to do this—just be sure to do it!

On the facing page is an example I found on a label and graphic artwork disc. Using my photo-editing software, I manipulated the label to the size and shape I needed; then I typed over the top to add the history, the maker, the quilter, the date, and the size. I printed it on 5″ × 7″ photo-transfer fabric, folded under the edges, and backed it with paper-backed fusible adhesive. (I prefer Heat'n Bond from Therm O Web.) I fused the label to the back of my quilt to hold it in place and then attached it permanently using a buttonhole stitch (page 29).

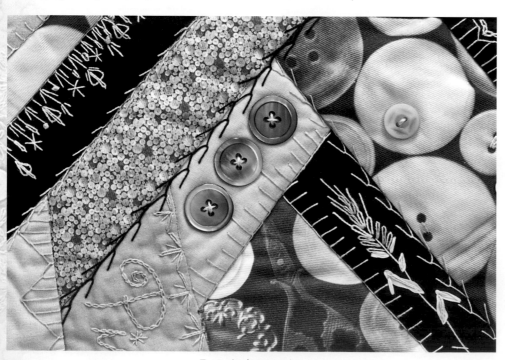

Teeny-tiny button print

Example of quilt label

Design and Layout

Layout Options

I have used a variety of block styles in my quilts. Each layout has its advantages and creates a distinct feel. *For the Love of Mother* is a single-block quilt, which allows more area for embellishing. *A Family Legacy* has smaller blocks assembled with sashing. Although this leaves less room for embellishment, the embellishment is more detailed and refined, giving the quilt a more intimate feel. Examples of other block styles you may want to try are the three-block table runner (*Children of the Past*) or wallhanging (*Timeless Memories*). The possibilities are infinite.

The block style can affect the feel of the crazy quilt. For example, using a four-sided photo in a block creates the look of a more traditional Log Cabin, as in *Ladies of the Past*. Using a five-sided picture and tilting it creates the look of a more traditional crazy quilt, as in *For the Love of Mother*.

For the Love of Mother

Children of the Past

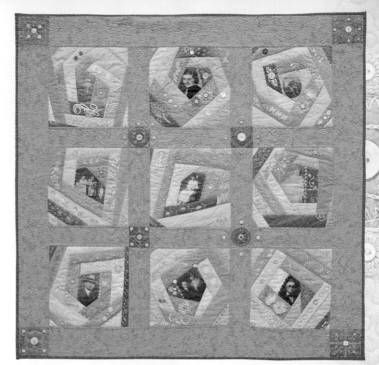

A Family Legacy

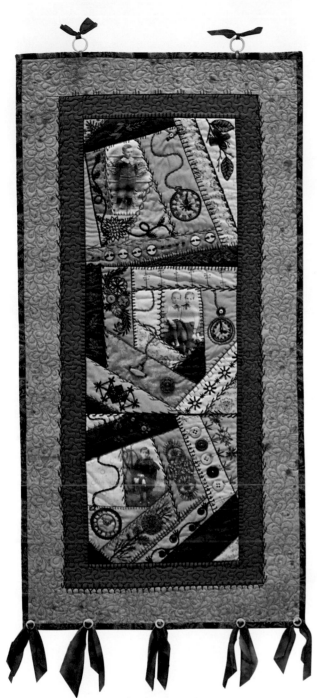

Timeless Memories

Ladies of the Past

Tip

For more random-looking blocks, trim your photo to give it five sides. Then you can add the fabric strips in a spiral direction around the photographs to create a more random, crazy-quilt style. Let the picture dictate the best cropping area and which sides should be cut off.

Stylizing

Notice the arrangement of the photographs in the three blocks of *Timeless Memories* (page 50). The left-right-left pattern creates a nice flow. Just like when reading a book, your eye moves from the left to the right. So even though the quilt has a more random look, it still has a pleasing flow. Of course, you may choose to put all your photographs in the center of the blocks, but the offset shown here adds to the overall crazy-quilt style.

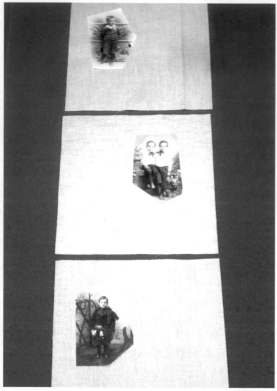

Photographs arranged on three muslin foundations.

A note about planned randomness: You'll notice that in the pictures of finished blocks and the finished quilt (page 50), the placement of the colored strips is balanced. So the randomness isn't truly random; it's planned, to a degree. Although there are no absolute rights and wrongs, you'll want to consider fabric placement when laying out each block to be sure there is balance. As you continue to work on the blocks, consider the fabric in the next block to be sure you continue the balance and flow through the entire project.

Some quilts are completely embroidered in all areas of the block. Others are only embroidered on the seams. Either option is fine. It's all about the style and look you want to create, which is sometimes dictated by the fabric or images you are using. Are you an antique look or a modern piece of art?

The fabric choice and the width of the border often make the style more obvious to the viewer. The wider the border, the more modern the look, I feel. If I were creating an antique feel, I would use multiple thinner borders. Sometimes a border doesn't have to be a single strip of fabric. Instead, it can be pieced to create another element in your design.

Detail of pieced border of *A Silken Tribute* (full quilt, page 70)

As an artist, I want to recognize Judith Baker Montano for her wonderful contribution to modern crazy quilting by developing The Montano Centerpiece Method. I've admired and been inspired by Ms. Montano's work for many years. I hope that I have "done her proud."

Foundation Piecing

Almost all the projects in this book are foundation pieced. I like this technique because it conserves fabric and allows me to trim any angle without worrying about the bias. The muslin foundation stabilizes the fabric strips and prevents stretching.

1. Arrange the photographs.

2. Pin each photo to the muslin backing.

3. Starting on any side, place the first strip of fabric, right side down, on the photograph.

4. Cut the new strip of fabric so the length completely covers the side of the photograph. Before cutting, check the length one more time to make sure the side of the photograph is completely covered.

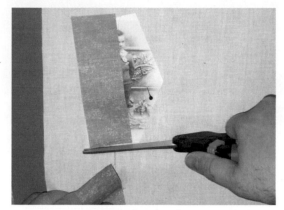
Cut strip to length.

5. Using a ¼″ seam, stitch along the edge of the 2 pieces of fabric, attaching them to the muslin foundation. Because you'll be sewing over the ends of the seams again with subsequent seams, there's no need to backstitch at the beginning and end of each seam.

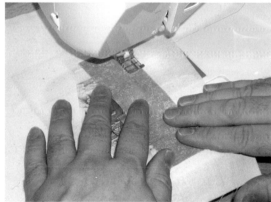
Stitch.

6. Press the piece after adding each new strip of fabric. This is important! Don't get lazy and wait until you finish all the piecing. Pressing after sewing each seam will keep your work straight and flat, the finished piece will look professional, and your work will be easier to manage. If you do not press, the piece will not lie right.

Push the iron away from you and over the seam to flatten out the work. *Do not stretch the fabric* or press down on the iron as though trying to push it through the table! Remember, this is fabric you're working with, not steel. Slowly ironing over a seam is always better than speeding through with lots of force. Work from the center out to get the best results.

Tip

If the blocks become misshapen during the embellishment process, don't worry. Iron each block as flat as possible to help straighten it out. Press both sides of the piece. It's okay to press over the hand stitching because the goal is to give the piece a timeworn feel. If your stitching and embellishments are fairly dimensional, however, you may want to use a pressing cloth.

7. Add the next strip of fabric. Be sure it's long enough to cover the next edge of the photograph and the width of the fabric added previously.

The example piece is being assembled in a counterclockwise direction. It makes no difference whether you work clockwise or counterclockwise. However, I've found that if you continue an entire block in the same direction, it will lie better and have a more pleasing flow.

Add next strip.

8. Press after adding each piece, always starting at the center of the photo and pressing out. Do not stretch or pull the fabric. Use a hot, dry iron to press the fabric flat.

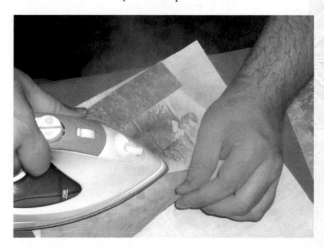

9. Clip the excess fabric from behind the overlapping pieces to a ¼″ seam allowance. This removes as much bulk as possible without getting so close to the seams that they might unravel. Piecing the rest of the block should go fairly quickly once you get the rhythm. This is a great technique for beginning quilters. It's simple and quick and doesn't involve a lot of intricate measuring or rotary cutting.

Note

When embroidering the blocks, you'll be thankful that you aren't sewing through the extra fabric. It's much easier to push the embroidery needle through just the foundation muslin and one piece of the top fabric.

10. Add the next strip of fabric, press, and trim. Continue until the entire muslin foundation is covered. Notice the progression of the pieces as they spiral out and around the photograph. The pie-shaped pieces contribute to the crazy quilt's random look. The last strips will run off the edges of the foundation muslin square, which will ensure that the block is completely covered. Don't worry about the sloppy ends. They'll be trimmed off in a minute.

11. Check to make sure that no slivers of the foundation fabric are showing at any of the edges. If they are, add more strips of fabric to cover them.

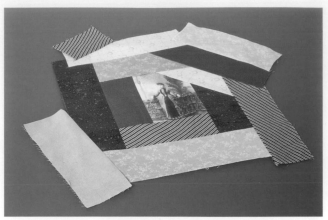

Completely cover foundation.

Squaring and Finishing Blocks

For a nice, smooth piece of textile art, it's important to square the blocks before assembling them.

1. Using any square ruler, trim each block to the desired size.

If the foundation fabric has shrunk a little from being handled, don't worry. Just make sure you end up with square blocks all the same size (that is, all the sides are the same length and all the corners are 90°). This might mean that a few places will have no foundation backing at the edge, but that's okay.

Trim blocks square.

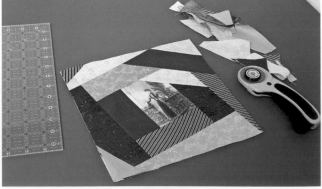

Trimmed block

2. Use a serger or sewing machine to stitch a scant ¼″ from the raw edge to finish each block. This will stabilize the loose ends of the fabric. It will also help the block remain square while you stitch embroidery and add embellishments.

Finished block

Pin blocks.

Note

Blocks can be embellished before or after they are sewn to each other. If you embellish before they are sewn together, you will still need to embellish the connecting seams after the quilt top is assembled.

Sewing Blocks Together without Sashing

1. After completing the embroidery and embellishing (pages 22–38), pin 2 of the blocks together, lining up the outer edges.

Note

If one block is slightly larger than the other, try to distribute the excess fabric equally along the length of the seam by pinning every 2″ or so and placing a bit of the extra fabric between each set of pins. For the projects in this book, if the difference is less than ½″, it can be eased in; but if it's more than ½″, you will have to trim it more accurately.

2. Stitch the blocks together.

3. Repeat Steps 1 and 2 to add more blocks.

Sashing and Borders

Sashing and borders are added basically the same way as sewing the blocks together.

Sashing can set off the blocks while allowing some elbow room between them so they can stand on their own (see *Button, Button, Who's Got the Button?* on page 63). Or it can add a unifying element to scrappy blocks. Borders add a finishing touch to a quilt, like a frame around a painting. Both sashing and borders provide another opportunity for creativity.

Sashing

1. Cut strips to the desired width of the sashing plus ½″ for seam allowances.

2. Ideally, all your blocks are the same siz; if not, make sure all the blocks are square and within ½″ of the same size. Measure each block through the center. Take the average and cut the short sashing strips to this length.

Tip

Be sure to take the measurement in the middle of the block, not on the outside edge; otherwise, the corners will flare.

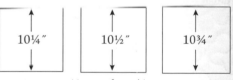

Measure for sashing.

3. Stitch the short sashing strips between the blocks to form rows; press the seam allowances toward the sashing. 4. Measure the length of each row (through the center). Take the average and cut the long sashing strips to this length.

5. Mark the center of each sashing strip and row. Match the ends, pin about every 2″, and stitch, easing in any fullness.

6. Align the rows of blocks and pin the bottom of the sashing strip to the top of the next row. Be sure to line up the short sashing strips.

7. Stitch, easing in any fullness.

8. Press the seam allowances toward the sashing.

Borders

If you have a flimsy cotton fabric, you may want to interface it to give it body and make a nice, smooth, flat border. I often use a linen or cotton upholstery fabric, which gives the border more body. Use the following technique to get a square quilt that lies flat and doesn't flare at the corners.

1. Cut strips to the desired width of the borders plus ½″ for seam allowances.

2. Place 2 border strips down the middle of the length of the quilt. Use a straightedge and rotary cutter to trim both the bottom and top edges of the border even with the top and bottom of the quilt.

Note

By placing both pieces of fabric down the middle of the quilt, you will know the borders are exactly the same length.

Trim border strips.

3. Pin a border strip to the front of the quilt with right sides together, starting with a pin at each end and pinning toward the middle. If either the quilt or the border piece is longer than the other, work the excess between the pins, so that any extra length is spread out along the entire seam.

Pin border.

4. Sew the border onto the quilt using a ¼″ seam allowance. Press the seam allowance toward the border. Repeat for the opposite side of the quilt.

5. For the top and bottom borders, place the border strips across the middle of the width of the quilt, which now includes the 2 vertical borders. Trim both ends of the border fabric to the exact measurement.

Trim top and bottom borders.

6. Sew the remaining borders onto the quilt using a ¼″ seam allowance. Press the seam allowance toward the borders.

Binding

The French miter is my favorite binding technique. It's easy and neat!

1. Cut enough 2″ strips to make a binding long enough to go around the piece, with at least 15″ extra for piecing the strips and overlapping the ends.

Don't use the selvage! Trim the selvage before piecing the binding strips together. It has no "give" and will not make a smooth binding.

2. Pin the strips right sides together at right angles and stitch diagonally to create a long, continuous strip.

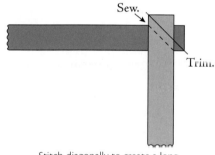

Stitch diagonally to create a long, continuous strip.

3. Trim the seam allowances to ¼″ and press the seams open.

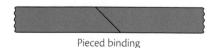

Pieced binding

4. Fold the binding in half lengthwise with wrong sides together; press.

5. Unfold and cut the end at a 45° angle. Press the cut edge under ¼″ and refold the strip.

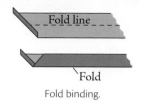

Fold binding.

6. Start in the middle of a side of the quilt (never a corner). I usually start near the bottom of the quilt. Align the binding with the quilt so all the raw edges are flat together. Leaving at least 2″ of the end of the binding loose, begin sewing with a ¼″ seam allowance.

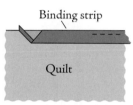

Position binding and stitch.

7. Stop stitching ¼″ from the corner. Clip the thread and remove the quilt from the sewing machine.

8. Fold the binding strip up and away from the corner of the quilt at 45°.

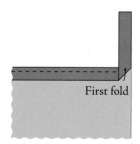

Fold binding up.

9. Fold the binding down, so it's even with the raw edge of the quilt.

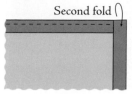

Fold binding down.

10. Begin sewing ¼″ from the upper edge and continue around the quilt, mitering all 4 corners.

11. As you approach the point where you started, trim the end of the binding, leaving it long enough to tuck inside the beginning of the binding. The 2 ends should overlap by about 1″. Stitch the rest of the binding to the quilt.

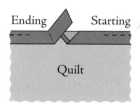

Ending binding

12. Turn the folded edge of the binding to the back of the quilt and hand sew it in place. Make sure the miters on the back look the same as they do on the front. Press.

Embellishing

I love embellishments. I am always on the lookout for possibilities, and you should be too. Be creative. Look for things that vary in scale, texture, body, and the overall look. Feel free to change your mind. If you sew something and you don't like the way it looks or the way it sits on the quilt, take your scissors and cut it off. Use your artist's creative judgment.

Trims

A trim is anything you can use to embellish. Some examples are ribbon, rickrack, lace, iron-on embroidery pieces, felt, and even scrapbooking embellishments.

In *A Silken Tribute* (page 70), I created the flowers on the borders from organza ribbon spray dyed with Brian's Aging Mist. Then I scorched the flowers with an iron to age them. I appliquéd the flowers on the border and held them down with beading and stitching.

You will see a white pearl and lace appliqué (originally meant for a wedding dress) in *For the Love of Mother* (page 53). Because this trim seemed too bright for the project, I hit it with ivory paint to antique and dull it before adding it. My Grandpa Peery blocks on *A Family Legacy* (page 67) sports an iron-on appliqué I found in a discount bin that I cut apart, ironed on, and reconfigured to make it flourish.

Dyed organza flower

Detail of Grandpa Peery Block 1

Something I have found fun to incorporate in my designs is fabulous findings from field trips to the scrapbook store. Charms with wonderful words such as *promise*, *always*, and *forever* really speak to me about my family. During one field trip, I found metal letter initials "B" and "H," which are my initials. They had such an Old World quality, I just had to use them.

Button bee

I love to use buttons to make insects (ladybugs, bumblebees, dragonflies). I made this bee from one oval shell button and two round shell buttons. I stitched over the top of the buttons with #8 perle cotton, and a large organza ribbon became the bee's gossamer wings.

Heart-shaped pearl buttons can be used many different ways, especially if the front is shiny and the back is matte. Stitch on top of them to make leaves. Four together with the point turned in make a dogwood blossom. Turn the points out to make a clover flower.

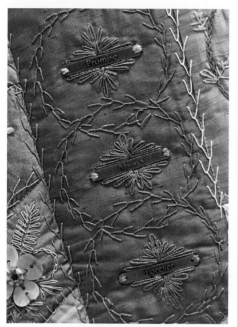
Scrapbook charms

Buttons

My use of buttons has expanded over the years. I started using brass, modern pearl, and glass buttons from local craft and sewing stores. Then I moved to scrapbooking stores, where I discovered matte-finish nylon buttons that come in many dyed colors and create an Old World look.

Scrapbooking stores are a great source for unique things with their own style. And now these stores have taken me into the realm of collector. I collect antique buttons and sort and use them not only for texture but also for style and interest to add history and elegance to my designs. (Be careful—you will need a 12-step program to get away from the button-collecting bug!)

Heart-shaped pearl buttons

The heart shape of these buttons is also perfect for ivy foliage, as in *A Silken Tribute* (page 70).

Beads

Beading is not for the fearful. It takes patience and persistence. Let me warn you: there will be a lot of "sweeper food." I know from experience that it's no fun to dig beads out of a vacuum bag! For *A Silken Tribute* (page 70), I loved the sheen of the silk and felt that it needed an elegant touch, so I started adding beads.

Tip

Make a story card when you're working on a project. A story card is a 3" × 5" card of scraps from each fabric used in the quilt. You can carry this card on your shopping excursion to match buttons, beads, and so on, with great ease.

I designed this beading to give the look of early 1800s beading and the quilts of that time, re-creating old designs with new things. I bought beads in my color palette of bronze and robin's-egg blue. I used many beads, sewing up through a button, adding the bead, then sewing back down through the button to create a center to a flower. I made other beading embellishments from matte and shiny textured beads to create the body of the dragonfly, the initials, the laurel wreaths, and the garlands.

Beading

Just a few beads can create dimension that otherwise wouldn't be present. The mix of beads will create visual interest and never leave you bored. Don't limit yourself to traditional beads. Your bead store will have charms, medallions, carved stones, and carved bone; all of these can create and inspire a design.

Jewelry

Consider adding your grandmother's locket or wedding ring, or a button from her favorite dress. Use any items that might add a special touch or that are personal to your family. Don't be afraid to consider using personal items as trim for your masterpiece. In *A Family Legacy* (page 67), I took the big pearly white dangles off a pair of earrings and embroidered across the top of them to create an entirely new design.

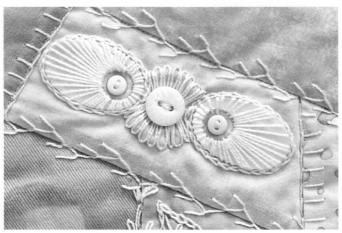

Detail of Grandpa Peery Block 2 from *A Family Legacy* (full quilt, page 67)

You can also pin your grandmother's favorite brooch to your quilt, giving it a place of honor while still allowing it to be removed and worn. What a neat way to use a special piece of jewelry! The possibilities are endless.

Artistic Flair

I provided a number of drawings in the Design Inspiration section (pages 86–94) to start your creative juices!

Stitching Techniques

Design and Drawing

Draw the designs for your hand embroidery work onto the finished block or quilt top (I use a #2 pencil). Refer to the designs on pages 86–94 and throughout the book for ideas and inspiration.

Note

I prefer to use a #2 pencil on light fabrics. I can see it better on the fabric, it's the way my grandma taught me, and it has always worked. I use a white pencil on dark fabrics.

Use found objects as a basis for your patterns. Look in Grandma's sewing basket for spools and buttons to draw around. In kitchen cabinets are cups, jar lids, and spice tins. Open the drawer to find spoons and maybe a wire potato masher (great for making an S-shaped ripple). If you look around, you'll probably see any number of things that have pleasing shapes. Using the shapes of everyday items will also result in a more primitive feel.

Found objects

If you have them, use your stencils or quilting templates for embroidery designs. By embroidering and chain stitching, you can create a look that is totally different from designs sewn with quilting stitches or painted. A template does not have to fit the space you have; it can run over the seamlines to create visual interest.

Start your design by drawing the larger shapes and then fill in the blanks with smaller details.

Trace around a large button for the larger center circle and then add some half-circle arcs using the edge of a spool.

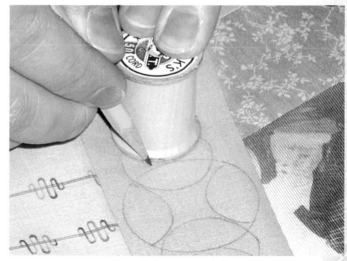

Draw circles to create design.

There's no need to plan the entire piece before you start sewing. Create any random design that is pleasing to you and let the design develop naturally. If you focus on one block at a time, the task won't seem as daunting.

Keep in mind that you'll want to balance the overall look of the piece. Strive for balance and randomness by combining circles with angles and busy, intricate patterns with simple straight lines.

Design Elements with Brian—No Rules! No Boundaries!

Balance can be symmetrical or asymmetrical. Here are some examples to try:

- Draw a circle in the middle of a piece (symmetry).

- Draw some different sizes of circles inside the first circle (asymmetry).

- Create two sweeping vines that start at a point between the shapes.

- Add a few leaves to finish the design. The bottom of each leaf should touch the vine.

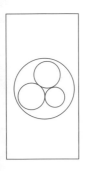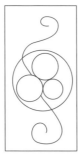

Draw design.

The easiest way I've found to create a symmetrical design (in which each half is a mirror image of the other half) is to take a piece of paper and fold it in half. Working from the fold out, draw a swirl, leaf, or any design, and cut it out. Open it up and you have a symmetrical template. If you don't like it, throw it away and start over. Position the template on the quilt and trace the design. Voilà! Complete artistic freedom with minimal supplies and expense.

To create the pocket watches in *Timeless Memories* (page 50), I drew a large circle with a small top loop. Later, I chain-stitched a simple line to create the watch fob. In one block, I also added a large flourish with some leaves in the lower left. Notice that some of these designs run over the seams of the different fabrics, adding to the random look. Always allow yourself to have fun and be playful with your designs. Allow freedom. This is crazy quilting.

Drawn designs.

Hand embroidery stitches add texture and contrast to a design. Compare the two embroidered and embellished blocks with the plain block below. Notice what a difference the embroidery makes. Adding embroidery and embellishment will add a random but finished look to a simple pieced block. By the time you finish the embroidery, the block will be a unified piece of art.

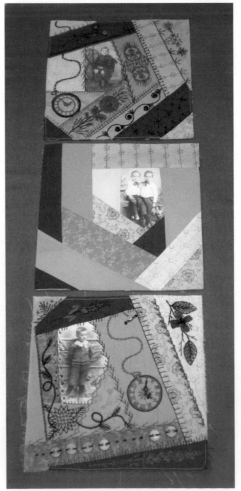

One plain and two embellished blocks.

Use a child's building block to draw three overlapping squares, creating a geometric shape. Fill in the blanks with a combination of chain stitches (page 28) and lazy daisies (page 29) to create a design. Let your stitches wander around the fabric; you'll love the results. Once you're happy with one end of the design, make a mirror image on the other end. It will look like you took hours to plan a design that really started with simple squares and then grew.

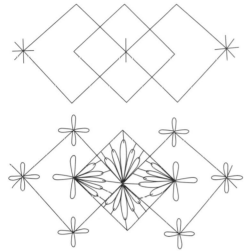

Design using child's building block

In the block shown below is a flourish, a spiral of circles, and a feather. This design started with some simple shapes and became a fill-in-the-blank exercise using basic embroidery stitches. This elaborate-looking motif is the result of combining simple stitches around simple shapes. Be playful and enjoy the process!

Detail of *Timeless Memories* (full quilt, page 50)

Simple shapes, elaborate motif

I combined buttons with lazy daisies and featherstitches, and borders with French knots, buttonhole stitches, and chain stitches (see Basic Stitches, pages 28–31). Once you've learned the stitches, it's all about trying different combinations. Be playful, try new things, and if you don't like the result, pick up the scissors and pull out the threads. Sometimes it just isn't successful the first time.

Ignoring the boundaries of the fabric pieces and crossing the seamlines will allow you to be more creative and give your imagination more options. This is not a precise art form. It's all about your creative freedom.

Crossing seamlines

Threads

I doodle with thread. Threads add texture, life, and contrast to a quilt. I use many different sizes and types of thread. One of my favorites is #8 perle cotton. I also like the texture and clean lines of crochet floss. I often use one thread through the whole project to help unify the colors throughout the work.

Basic Stitches

All of these stitches, with the exception of the Japanese ribbon stitch, can be created from assorted threads or ribbon (silk, cotton, or organza). The Japanese ribbon stitch can only be made with ribbon.

Work through your own creative process to place the stitches wherever you choose, using colors that will give your project the perfect look. I'm merely showing you stitches and the many interpretations that can come from them. What you do with them is entirely up to you.

Soft Knot

A soft knot on the back of the work will stay close to the fabric, will not misshape the project, and won't leave all those running threads on the back. If you're mixing threads, they can catch on the back and create a real mess. When the designs get complex, you don't want to sew through all those running threads.

1. Come up at A (on the back side of the project) and wrap the thread over the top of the needle to create a loop.

2. Pull the needle and thread in one direction and the loop in the other direction to create a Y.

3. Place your finger in the middle of the Y and pull the thread through until it finishes in a knot under your nail.

4. Trim the thread about ¼" from the knot.

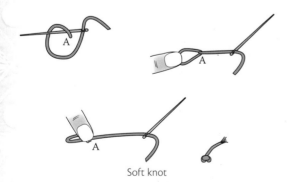

Soft knot

French Knot

Uses of the French knot are endless. What a versatile stitch! It's great for creating flower centers, clusters of grapes, texture to fill an area around flowers, baby's breath from a featherstitch, and so much more. You will want to add this stitch to your repertoire.

1. Come up at A and wrap the thread twice around the needle.

2. While tilting the needle one way and holding the thread the other way, go down at B (as close to A as possible) and keep the thread close to the fabric.

3. Hold the knot in place while pulling the needle through the fabric.

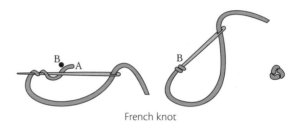

French knot

Chain Stitch

You can make this stitch in any direction—up or down, left or right. You can also shape it to fit a curved line.

1. Come up at A and go down at B (close to A). Make a loop and hold the loop in place with your thumb. Come up at C inside the loop. Always keep the loop to the forward point of the needle so you can direct the loop in the line you want to travel.

2. Pull the needle taut, but not so tight that you lose the nice soft loop. Create the same stitch again, but this time, do it inside the loop to continue the chain.

Chain stitch

Lazy Daisy

I love to use lazy daisy flowers with button embellishments and French knots in the center. Look carefully at the detail photo of *Children of the Past* (page 48) and you'll see a large circle surrounded by lazy daisies to create a sunflower.

1. Come up at A and go down at B (close to A). Make a loop and hold the loop in place with your thumb. Come up at C. (However large you want the daisy petal to be is how far you want to travel—usually ⅛″–¼″.)

2. Pull and leave a nice, loopy, billowed arch to create a petal.

3. Go straight down on the other side of the loop at D, creating a small stitch to tack the loop in place. You've now made your first daisy petal. Go back to the center to create more of these in concentric shapes and make as many petals as you want.

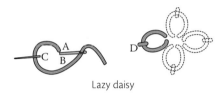

Lazy daisy

Brian's Y Stitch

Seldom will you use this stitch by itself. But in combination, it's a great tool to tie many stitches together. Some examples are the detailed leaf (page 32), the cotton ribbon medallion (page 37), and the woven pinwheel flower (page 32).

1. Come up at A, go down at B, and come up at C.

2. Cross under the first stitch and go down at D, creating a Y.

The modified Y stitch, or star stitch, is the same as the Y stitch but with a short stem to create the star effect.

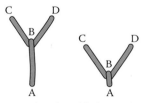

Y stitch and modified Y stitch

Brian's Asterisk

Use this stitch to incorporate background texture and patterns or to make flowers. It's very simple, yet very effective.

1. Make 2 straight stitches across each other to create a cross.

2. Add 2 straight stitches to make an X across the cross, creating the asterisk.

3. Bring the needle up in the center of the asterisk and take a tack stitch across all 4 threads.

Brian's asterisk

Buttonhole Stitch

The buttonhole stitch is one of the most diverse stitches you will learn. By varying the size and direction, you can create many things from this one marvelous stitch. I use this stitch to appliqué for a primitive look, to outline, or to give ornamental stitching to seams. Stitch at an angle to create a fern effect.

1. Come up at A and travel over and down at B. Hold the thread between A and B loosely, and come up at C.

2. Continue, pulling each stitch evenly taut. Keep the stitches even and in a straight line.

Buttonhole stitch

I usually use the buttonhole stitch along a seam. However, it can also double as a decorative stitch—just draw a line and stitch away.

Buttonhole stitch variations

Outline/Stem Stitch

Use the stem stitch to write or to make intricate lines.

1. Come up at A, take a small stitch, and go down at B; then come up at C about halfway back to A.

2. Travel half a stitch, go down at D, and come up at E (right next to B). Continue, keeping the thread to the bottom and the needle to the top to make a nice, even stem. Always make sure the thread is on the same side of the needle as you travel.

Outline/stem stitch

Cretan

This even stitch creates a nice balance down a center seam.

1. Imagine 3 vertical lines. (If this is a new stitch for you, go ahead and draw 3 vertical lines on your fabric with a removable marker, such as a chalk pencil.) Come up at A. Make a stitch from B to C with the thread under the needle without stitching all the way to the center line.

2. Pull the thread through. Make the next stitch the same as in Step 1, but go down at D and come up at E (from left to right).

3. Repeat Steps 1 and 2, alternating from side to side.

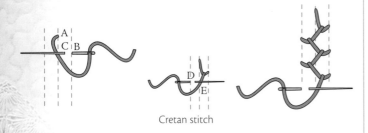

Cretan stitch

Featherstitch

This is one of my favorite stitches to use in crazy quilts. It helps create the Old World style. It's also a versatile stitch. But be aware—it's a directional stitch! The line does not have to be straight! You could also follow a seam, which is where this stitch is most prominently used in quilts. Using a seamline helps keep the stitches straight and consistent.

1. Come up at A, go down at B, and come up at C.

2. Alternate the stitches back and forth on each side of an imaginary line.

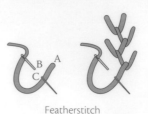

Featherstitch

The double featherstitch is created the same as the featherstitch; you just do 2 stitches before alternating on either side of the imaginary line.

To form a triple featherstitch, guess what? Just do 3 stitches before alternating on either side of the imaginary line!

The illustration has a few ideas to get you started.

Double featherstitch   Triple featherstitch   Circular featherstitch

Uneven single featherstitch   Uneven single featherstitch with Lazy Daisies and French Knots   Double featherstitch with French Knots

Japanese Ribbon Stitch

When making the Japanese ribbon stitch, you will want to use ribbon. Thread creates a big, hot mess!

Come up at A. With your thumb, place the silk ribbon horizontal to where you want the foliage or petal to go. Pierce the ribbon with your needle at B, pulling gently to the back until the ribbon turns in gracefully on itself, making the first Japanese ribbon stitch.

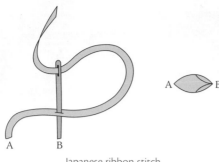

Japanese ribbon stitch

Use multiple Japanese ribbon stitches to create foliage and flowers, as shown. This is a useful stitch!

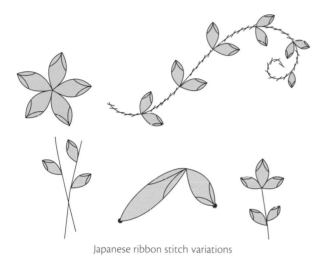

Japanese ribbon stitch variations

Combination Stitches

Double-Tacked Lazy Daisy Flower

Hey, folks! This stitch is about geometry. Sometimes when you are designing, you need an angular, square flower to break up all the soft, round lines. This flower creates that edginess.

1. Draw a circle.

2. Come up at A and make a loop. Go down at B (right next to A) and come up at C (inside the loop). Go down at D to create a tiny tack stitch over the loop.

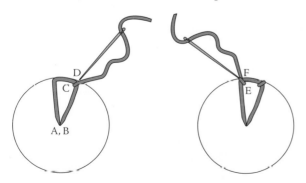

3. Come up at E and go down at F to create a square petal.

4. Repeat Steps 2 and 3 until you create a flower with as many petals as you choose.

5. To finish the design, come up in the center and take a stitch halfway down the length of each petal.

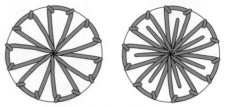

Double-tacked lazy daisy flower

Fishbone with Center Rib Stitch

Creating a skeletal system on a leaf is an easy, effective way to add detail, excitement, and depth.

1. Trace around a bone folder (or draw your own elongated figure) to mark the shape that will guide your stitches.

2. Take a long stitch for the center rib from the base (A) to the tip (B)—the full length of the shape.

3. Bring the needle up at C and go down at D.

4. Bring the needle up at E and go down at F.

5. Repeat Steps 3 and 4 until the shape is filled.

6. Add a chain stitch (page 28) to outline the finished shape. The chain stitch should go in the same direction on each side of the shape for a pleasing flow.

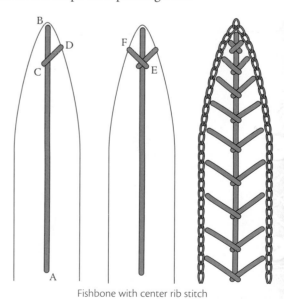

Fishbone with center rib stitch

Detailed Leaf

Use the detailed leaf individually or in multiples. If you use leaves in a grouping, detail some while leaving others simple to create interest and texture and to make the leaves appear tilted and shadowed.

1. Sketch a leaf shape.

2. Come up at A and go down at B to create the leaf's center vein.

3. Come up at C and go down at D.

4. Come up at E, go under the stitch made in Step 3, and go down at F to create a Y stitch.

5. Repeat Steps 3 and 4 to create alternating Y stitches on each side of the leaf's center vein.

6. Outline the leaf with a chain stitch (page 28). The chain stitch should go in the same direction on each side of the leaf, always heading for the top.

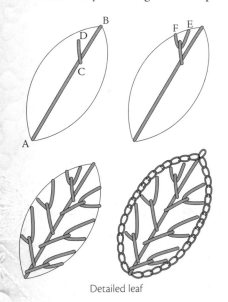

Detailed leaf

Woven Pinwheel Flower

1. Come up at A, go down at B, and come up at C. Cross under the AB stitch and go down at D, creating a Y.

2. Come up at E, cross under threads D and C, and go down at F, creating spokes.

3. Come up in the center of the spokes. Weave the thread over and under the spokes in a circle until all the spokes are covered. You can go clockwise or counterclockwise, as long as you continue in the same direction.

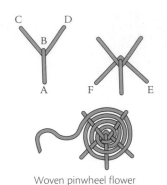

Woven pinwheel flower

Note

If you want a flower larger than ½", use a template to draw a circle to keep the spokes even. Larger designs may require more spokes. Create as many spokes as you want—just be sure the total number of spokes is uneven.

Lattice Sunflower

I am not a traditionalist in embroidery. I make long stitches and then tack them down. I like to simplify what's already been done. Sometimes I want a more detailed, refined design; other times I want to be bold and make a statement. Either can be done with this stitch combination. It can be shaped like a Fabergé egg or a basket. It's a versatile stitch!

1. Draw a circle.

2. Come up at A, go down at B, come up at C, go down at D, come up at E, go down at F, come up at G, and go down at H.

3. To create the lattice: Come up at I, go down at J, come up at K, go down at L, come up at M, go down at N, come up at O, and go down at P.

4. Cross the lattice: Come up at Q and go down at R. I know you're starting to get it. Repeat this step until you get to the end. Follow the arrows to complete the design on one side. Take the needle under the work and come up at S to cross the lattice on the other side in the same manner.

5. Cross the tacks to make X's.

6. Add lazy daisies (page 29) around the edge and voilà! You have a sunflower!

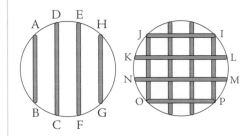

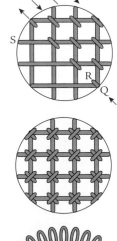

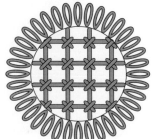

Lattice sunflower

Lattice sunflower variations

Baby's Breath

When you want something ethereal, use baby's breath. It's very open and delicate and can be combined with other stitches for dramatic effect.

1. Do a loose, uneven featherstitch (page 30) to create the shape of a stem.

2. Add French knots (page 28) to the ends of the stems, finishing each one off nicely.

Baby's breath variations

Larkspur

This simple stem is great when you need a long, vertical design in a narrow area. It gives nice visual relief and stays within the parameter of a single piece of fabric in the block.

1. Come up at A and go down at B to create a stem. Create tack stitches for the foliage as follows: come up at C, go down at D, come up at E, go down at F, come up at G, and go down at H. Tie a soft knot (page 28) on the back.

2. Using the Japanese ribbon stitch (page 30), create a natural-looking group of flowers at the top of the stem. You can accomplish this by alternating the number of petals and stitching flowers in an elongated teardrop shape.

3. With the ribbon still attached, fill in around the flowers with ribbon French knots (page 28). Increasing and decreasing the number of wraps around the needle for each knot will create a more natural look to the flowers. Using clusters of lazy daisies (page 29), with a small stitch extending from each, will create foliage at the tips of the branches. Add a few of these under the flowers to give the look of a calyx.

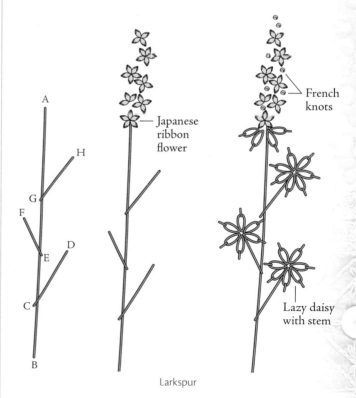

Larkspur

Bow

Use the Japanese ribbon stitch (page 30) to make a charming bow.

1. Start with 3 Japanese ribbon stitches to create a triangle. Come up at A, go down at B, come up at C, and go down at D to create a V shape. Take the needle under the fabric; then come up at E and go down at F to create one side of the bow.

2. Go back to the center and repeat Step 1 on the opposite side.

3. Put a French knot (page 28) in the center of the bow. Use the Japanese ribbon stitch to add tails.

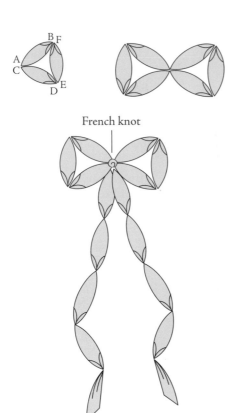

French knot

Bow

Note

I am frugal when it comes to my silk ribbon, and I don't like to waste it on the back. I take a small backstitch to create the next loop instead of traveling on the back. The silk ribbon fluffs over itself so I can't see the backstitch. I make sure to leave the ribbons loose and billowy to create a nice interpretation of a bow.

Stitched Medallion

The circle for this simple medallion was traced using a toilet paper roll.

1. Draw a circle where you want it. Place a small dot in the center of the circle. Place the edge of the roll (or other round object) on the center point in the direction you want the design to flow; draw a half-moon. Repeat 3 more times.

2. Begin stitching on the drawn lines. Chain stitch (page 28) on each spoke from the center out to create a nice flow for the medallion.

3. Between each chain-stitched petal, create a flourish of 3 lazy daisies (page 29) from the outside of the ring to the center. Make 5 straight stitches in the middle of each chain stitch petal to bring focus to the center of the medallion. Close the tops of the chain stitch petals with 3 buttonhole stitches (page 29). This now looks like an elaborate medallion, but how simple!

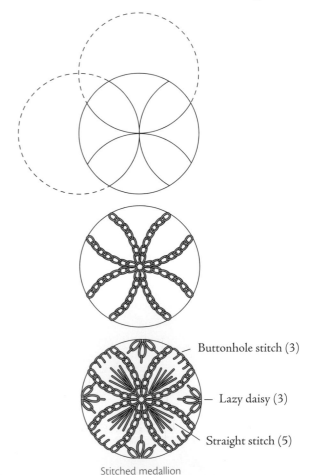

Buttonhole stitch (3)

Lazy daisy (3)

Straight stitch (5)

Stitched medallion

Wheat Stem

In the real world of stitchery, traveling 3″–4″ is a no-no. But I say all rules are meant to be broken.

STEMS

1. Come up at A, travel the distance you want the length of the stem to be, and go down at B. Move slightly to the side and down; come up at C. Travel parallel to the first line and go down at D to create 2 parallel lines. Travel from D and come up at E. Cross the 2 parallel lines and end at F. Tie a soft knot (page 28) on the back.

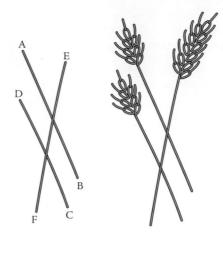

BEARD TOPS

The most important thing is to keep the beards (lazy daisy stitches with elongated tack stitches, page 29) parallel to each other and side by side. Start at the top of one of the stems. Tilt the lazy daisy stitch slightly to the right or the left, depending on which side you choose to start.

2. When tacking down the loop of the lazy daisy stitch, take a long stitch to create a long beard. Continue to make parallel beards across from each other. An uneven number is more interesting.

3. After you've made as many hulls as you need, put one directly in the middle of the last 2 hulls to end the wheat beard, creating a point at the end of your stalk of wheat.

4. Continue to create a bunch of wheat at the top of each stem.

FOLIAGE

5. Add Japanese ribbon stitch foliage (page 30). Use these stitches to tack down the long wheat stalks.

Wheat stem

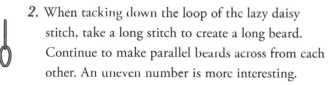

Note

I often use the same color of thread and same color of silk ribbon to create a monochromatic scheme, but you can use as much color as you like.

Flower Patch

The flower patch gives you a very intricate element with movement and visual interest, and yet it won't overpower anything around it.

STEMS

Three long lines at different lengths will give a wildflower look.

1. Come up at A, go down at B, come up at C, go down at D, come up at E, and go down at F. Tie a soft knot (page 28) on the back.

2. Create long stitches over the first 3 long lines to hold them down. Come up at G, go down at H, come up at I, go down at J, come up at K, and go down at L. Come up at M and go back down at the top of L. Come up at I and go down at N.

BLOOMS

3. Create a tall, linear grouping of French knots (page 28) that is wider toward the bottom and that tapers to a point at the top. Increasing the number of times you wrap the thread around the needle toward the bottom of the flower while decreasing toward the top will give a nice, conical shape. At the tip of each flower, take 3–5 running stitches that taper the flower even more, giving it a delicate, refined line. To complete the bloom, use Japanese ribbon stitches (page 30) at the bottom, varying the number from 3–6 for a natural effect.

FOLIAGE

4. To create the foliage and tack the main stems, use Japanese ribbon stitches. Stitch these at an angle so they appear to be hanging naturally from the stem toward the ground. Use the same Japanese ribbon stitch at the bottom but with a much longer run to create reeds.

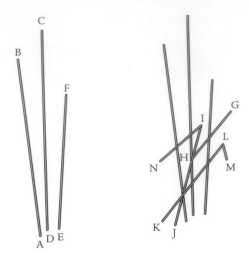

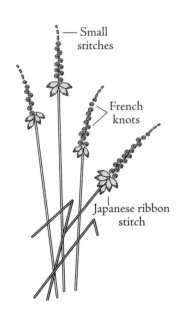

— Small stitches

French knots

Japanese ribbon stitch

Japanese ribbon stitch (foliage)

Japanese ribbon stitch (reed)

Flower patch

Cotton Ribbon Medallion

1. Use knotted double thread to sew a running stitch along one side of a 10″ length of ¾″-wide ribbon. I like the organic texture of cotton ribbon, which you can find in the scrapbook area of a hobby store and in the binding and bias tape area of a fabric store.

2. Pull the thread to gather the ribbon into a circle; tie off the thread. Tuck the raw ends to one side on the back of the ribbon and press the entire piece flat.

Ribbon gathered in circle

3. Position the ribbon on the quilt and sew it in place with Brian's Y stitch (page 29) using perle cotton thread.

4. Add 2 more spokes for a total of 5 (similar to the woven pinwheel flower, page 32).

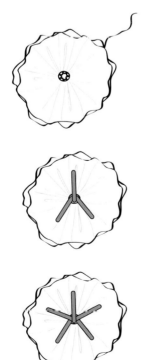

5. Bring the needle up at A, down at B, up at C, and down at D to create the first star point.

6. Repeat Step 5 at each spoke to tack down the medallion and create a star.

Cotton ribbon medallion

Completed cotton ribbon medallion

Felt appliqué

Felt Appliqué

Cut out random-shaped pieces (such as a circle or leaf) from wool or felt. Anyone can (and should) do this. Add stitching to these simple forms to add detail and dimension.

FLOWER

1. Start with any size circle of wool or felt.

2. To make a 6-petal flower, cut 6 evenly spaced slits in the circle (don't cut all the way to the center or your flower will fall apart!).

3. Round the corner of each petal by cutting off a small curve.

4. Appliqué the flower to your project with 3 straight stitches in each petal. You can add beads, French knots, or a button to the center to finish the look.

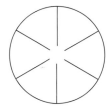 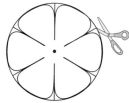 

Felt appliqué flowers

If your flower isn't completely tacked down, it's okay. This is a dimensional flower.

LEAF (FISHBONE)

1. Cut out a leaf shape from wool or felt. Cutting each leaf by hand means that each leaf will have a unique shape. It's a simple shape. No patterns needed!

2. Appliqué the leaf to your project with a single straight stitch through the center; this will become the center vein. Come up at A and go down at B.

3. Come up at C, go over the center rib, and go down at D. Alternate sides, always going over the center rib to tack it in place. (This applique stitch is similar to the fishbone with center rib stitch on page 31, but without the chainstitch around the edge.)

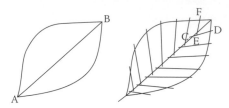

Fishbone felt appliqué leaf

LEAF (DETAILED)

1. Cut out a leaf shape by hand from wool or felt.

2. Appliqué the leaf to your project with a single straight stitch through the center; this will become the center vein. Come up at A and go down at B.

3. Come up at C and go down at D. Come up at E, go around D, and go down at F to create a Y stitch. Repeat, creating alternating Y stitches on each side of the leaf's center vein. (This applique stitch is similar to the Detailed Leaf stitch on page 32, but without the chain stitch around the edge.)

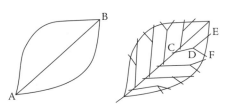

Detailed felt appliqué leaf

Great-Grandma's Pillow

Made by Brian Haggard | **Finished size:** 14″ × 14″

A picture of my great-grandmother inspired this easy pillow. I kept the borders simple to allow room for creating a handmade motif. This project is great for making a simple gift that is personalized for that very special family member or friend.

Materials

- Antique photograph printed on 8½″ × 11″ sheet of cotton twill PhotoFabric (CTPF) (see Selecting, Scanning, and Printing Photographs on Fabric, page 11)
- Golden beige fabric: ¾ yard for borders and pillow back
- Perle cotton #8 in soft gold: 1 skein
- Buttons: 19 mother-of-pearl or shell
- Wooden thread spool or other circular found objects to use as templates for embroidery
- Brian's Aging Mist (page 95)
- 14″ × 14″ pillow form

Cutting

FABRIC PHOTOGRAPH

- Fussy cut the photograph to 6½″ × 6½″.

BEIGE

- Cut 2 strips 4½″ × 6½″ for the top and bottom borders.
- Cut 2 strips 4½″ × 14½″ for the side borders.
- Cut 2 pieces 9″ × 14½″ for the pillow back.

Construction

Press after each step. Use a ¼″ seam allowance.

1. Sew the 4½″ × 6½″ top and bottom borders onto the 6½″ × 6½″ photograph; press. Add the 4½″ × 14½″ side borders.

2. Cover the face of the photograph with your hand to control overspray; spray the pillow top with Brian's Aging Mist. Unlike aging the borders prior to attaching them (page 10), this technique will give a soft edge to the spray texture.

3. Heat set using a pressing cloth and a hot, dry iron. Press until the fabric is dry.

Embellishment

1. Draw a design on the pillow. This will be your pattern to embroider. Eyeball it. Use a plate, cup, or something similar (approximately 5″ in diameter) as a template for the circles in each corner. I used a wooden spool as a template to create the clamshell shapes. Start at the center of the photograph and draw arches on each side. Bring the arches just to the edge of the pillow without crossing onto the seam allowances. Try for symmetry on all 4 sides.

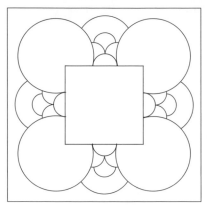

Embroidery design

2. Embroider the circles and around the photo using the featherstitch (page 30). Notice that the featherstitch goes in one direction to keep everything even and continuous. This gives a simple, quiet flow to the piece.

Stitch design

3. The clamshell designs are created using the buttonhole stitch (page 29), with a simple straight stitch at the base of the small arches.

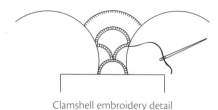

Clamshell embroidery detail

4. Sew on the buttons with #8 perle cotton. Notice how the buttons are attached to create the look of trim (decorative ornamental pieces) instead of buttons.

Pillow Construction

1. Fold under 1″ along a 14½″ side of each pillow backing piece.

2. Overlap the center edges of the pillow back pieces and place with right sides facing the right side of the pillow front, as shown. Pin and sew around all 4 sides. Turn right side out.

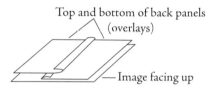

Top and bottom of back panels (overlays)

Image facing up

3. Place the pillow form inside.

4. Buttonhole stitch along the exposed edge of the pillow back.

5. Add 3 buttons along the center edge.

Finished pillow back

Ladies of the Past

found photos of these ladies while antiquing, and they became instant ancestors. I wanted this wallhanging to look like a timeless, faded piece of art. Although all the fabrics are new, I chose low-contrast, quiet patterns in neutral sepia tones (creams and beiges) to create this look. I love "altered art"—where I, or any artist, take ordinary everyday objects and use them in a new or unusual way to create a design, such as the keys used to hang the piece. I also used antique buttons and appliqué to create a worn, faded look and to add to the vintage appeal. Notice the placement of the photographs for harmony and balance: The subjects are looking gracefully from side to side, creating a peaceful coexistence.

Made by Brian Haggard | **Finished size:** 14″ × 32″

Materials

- 3 antique photographs printed on 8½″ × 11″ sheets of cotton twill PhotoFabric (CTPF) (Selecting, Scanning, and Printing Photographs on Fabric, page 11)

- Muslin: ½ yard for foundation

- Cotton prints: 6–10 fat eighths (11″ × 18″) in various neutral prints for foundation piecing

- Upholstery-weight cotton: ⅜ yard for borders

- Backing: ½ yard*

- Crochet cotton: 1 skein in ecru

- Buttons: 6–10 (antique, shell, or whatever you like)

- Keys: 2 for hanging

- Blue painter's tape

- Brian's Aging Mist (page 95)

- Wooden thread spools or other circular found objects to use as templates for embroidery

- Paper-backed fusible web: 12″ × 12″ for appliqués (I prefer Heat'n Bond Lite.)

* I like the quilt back to be a continuation of the visual style that I have created on the front, so I often choose a fabric used in the foundation piecing for the backing. I think this is the sort of thing that separates an "art piece" from traditional work.

Cutting

FABRIC PHOTOGRAPH

- Fussy cut the photographs to approximately 3″ × 5″ (let the photographs dictate the shape and size).

MUSLIN

- Cut 3 squares 9½″ × 9½″ for the block foundations.

- Cut 1 square 12″ × 12″ for the fusible appliqué embellishments.

COTTON PRINTS

- Cut randomly sized strips from 1½″ to 2½″ wide for the foundation piecing. Do this quickly by folding the fat eighths twice to create 4 layers of fabric and then cutting many strips in all different widths across the grain. Pile them up and use them for the foundation piecing.

UPHOLSTERY-WEIGHT COTTON

- Cut 2 strips 3″ × 9½″ for the top and bottom borders.

- Cut 2 strips 3″ × 32½″ (at least) for the side borders.

BACKING

- Cut a rectangle 14½″ × 32½″.

Construction

Press after each step.

1. Pin the 3 photographs to the muslin foundation pieces. Arrange the photographs to put the design in motion. Notice how the subjects are facing into the piece and are placed on alternating sides of the wallhanging.

2. Use the cotton print strips to foundation piece the first block; trim to 9½″ × 9½″ (Foundation Piecing, pages 16–19).

3. Foundation piece and trim Block 2. Note the placement of the fabric strips in Block 1 as you foundation piece Block 2; try to alternate the placement of light and dark strips in each block to create rhythm and balance throughout.

Note

Directional fabrics need to be used in the direction they are intended. One of my pet peeves is seeing a beautiful work in which all the designs are haphazard. An art quilt will be viewed from one direction on the wall, and this direction should be considered in the creative process.

4. Foundation piece and trim Block 3.

5. Sew the 3 blocks together.

Embellishment

1. Apply paper-backed fusible web to the back of the 12" × 12" square of muslin. Draw and cut out 3 circles 2½" in diameter (or any other shape you would like to use). You will use 1 appliqué circle for each block to create a backdrop for your hand stitching.

2. Place these circles on the wall-hanging where they look nice, crossing seamlines if necessary. Breaking lines creates impact, drama, and focal points. It's very artistic! Follow the manufacturer's instructions to fuse the circles to the quilt top. Use a buttonhole stitch (page 29) to appliqué them to the piece. The other circle details are made of stitches.

3. For the circle in the middle block, draw the leaves, smaller circles, and flower arc using a circle template such as a spool of thread or cup.

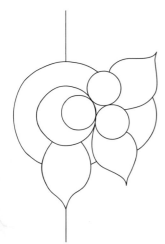

Appliquéd circles, drawn leaves, and arc

4. Continue to draw the scrolls.

Add scrolls.

5. For the circle in the third block, using the illustration for guidance, draw around a bone folder or other similar shape to draw the feather points.

Feather points

6. Add buttons. This will create the third of 3 balanced motifs.

Three balanced motifs

7. Add the hand embroidery. Be organic. There is no need to draw everything and follow the lines. Make a circle and come up with fabulous things to fill it. Use the lazy daisy (page 29), buttonhole (page 29), chain (page 28), Brian's Y stitch (page 29), and fishbone with center rib stitches (page 31). Add elements or components that appeal to you to make a unique design.

8. Create stitches on the seams as you wish. (Remember, when you're stitching close to a motif, you want to use a simple stitch, like a chain buttonhole stitch, so it doesn't get too busy and distract from the motifs.)

Finishing

1. Sew the 3″ × 9½″ top and bottom strips to the quilt top. Add the 3″ × 32½″ side border strips.

2. Place a piece of paper to cover everything except the borders (or cover whatever you don't want stained). Use blue painter's tape to hold the paper in place. Make sure the tape covers the piece right up to the edge of the borders.

3. Mist the entire border with water so that the stain will bleed. Spray the border with Brian's Aging Mist; press lightly on the spray bottle to get splatters. This makes the borders look aged and blends them with the rest of the piece. Remove the tape and paper. Heat set the stain by pressing the piece.

4. Sew the back to the front of the wallhanging, right sides together. Leave a 6″ opening along one side. Turn the piece right side out. Fold the seam allowances of the 6″ opening to the inside and press.

5. Topstitch ⅛″ all around the edge.

6. Topstitch ⅛″ outside the edge of each block.

7. Press the quilt and add the keys for hangers.

Sew ⅛″ outside each block.

Children of the Past

Made by Brian Haggard | **Finished size:** 46½″ × 18½″

In my antiquing travels, I found the wonderful photos of children from the 1800s that inspired this piece. The children seemed so pensive standing on their seats, waiting for me to find them. Notice how they are tilting slightly, which creates more visual interest. The piece is made with three 10″ × 10″ blocks, and only the seams of the blocks are embroidered. The fancy embroidery is done on 4″ × 10″ rectangles set on each side. Only one print fabric is used in this project. This is a nice-sized piece to take with you and work on in the car (but, please, not if you're driving!) or in the doctor's office.

When it's finished, set your beautiful runner in the middle of your table, invite some friends over for a nice cup of tea, and admire your work of art.

Materials

- 3 antique photographs printed on 8½" × 11" sheet(s) of cotton twill PhotoFabric (CTPF) (see Selecting, Scanning, and Printing Photographs on Fabric, page 11)
- Muslin: ½ yard for foundations
- Vintage upholstery fabric (54" wide): ½ yard for borders and foundation piecing
- Cranberry red satin (e.g., suit lining): ⅛ yard for foundation piecing
- Solids: ⅛ yard each of 2 coordinating fabrics for foundation piecing and ¼ yard for fancy embroidery and foundation piecing
- Backing and binding: 1½ yards
- Perle cotton #8 in soft gold, pink, raspberry, robin's-egg blue, and cream: 1 skein each
- #7 silk ribbon in olive green
- Wooden thread spool or other circular found objects to use as templates for embroidery
- Cotton batting: 50" × 21" (Use the thinnest you can find; I used Warm and Natural.)

Cutting

Honestly, I don't measure. I just lay out my fabric and cut it with a rotary cutter; wherever it lands, it lands. This makes it all more organic and *fun*! Nonetheless, here are the cutting instructions for all the traditionalists.

FABRIC PHOTOGRAPH
- Fussy cut the 3 photographs to 3½" × 5½".

MUSLIN
- Cut 3 squares 10½" × 10½" for the foundations.

VINTAGE UPHOLSTERY FABRIC
- Cut 1 strip 2" × fabric width for the foundation piecing.
- Cut 2 strips 4½" × 10½" for the side borders.
- Cut 2 strips 4½" × 46½" for the top and bottom borders.

CRANBERRY RED SATIN
- Cut a strip somewhere between 1" and 2" wide × fabric width for the foundation piecing.

SOLIDS
- Cut 2 strips 4½" × 10½" from the ¼ yard of solid cotton fabric. (One of these rectangles will be added to each side of the assembled blocks and will be embroidered.)
- Cut a strip 1"–2" wide × fabric width from each of the 3 solid fabrics for the foundation piecing.

BACKING AND BINDING
- Cut 50" × 21" for the backing.
- Cut 4 strips 2" × fabric width for the binding.

Construction

Press after each step. Use a ¼" seam allowance.

1. Pin the 3 photographs on the foundations, with 2 of the photos set at an angle. The angled photographs make the pieces look more random and create visual interest.

2. Use the solid, satin, and upholstery strips to foundation piece each block, creating the design as you go and making sure to never allow strips of the same fabric to touch. Keep adding the fabrics around the photograph, completely covering the foundation (See Foundation Piecing, page 16–19).

3. Press carefully.

Note

Press this piece from the back to avoid scorching the satin fabric. A hot iron is not a friend of polyester-blend fabrics.

4. Square the blocks to 10½" × 10½" and sew them together.

5. Sew a 4½" × 10½" solid strip to the left and right sides of the piece.

6. Add a 4½" × 10½" upholstery fabric border strip to the left and right sides; then add the 4½" × 46½" top and bottom borders.

Embellishment

It's time to embroider! I challenge you to be playful with your needle.

1. Trace the pattern (page 49) or create a design of your own. For more ideas, refer to Chapter 7: Stitching Techniques—Basic Stitches; Combination Stitches (pages 25–38).

2. Use the cretan stitch (page 30) with cream perle cotton to outline the blocks. Embroider the remaining seams, choosing different stitches to create random patterns.

For more embellishment designs see Design Inspiration (pages 86–94).

Finishing

1. Layer the top with the batting and backing; quilt as desired.

2. Add binding.

Embroidery

Seam embroidery

Embroidery pattern

Timeless Memories

Made by Brian Haggard, machine quilted by Melissa Taylor
Finished size: 20″ × 39″

I love pocket watches and am obsessed by time. The look of clocks and watches is something I use in a lot of my altered art and designs. I chose these photographs from my collection because they related to each other in terms of both subject and style. The fabrics were piled on my worktable from previous projects. When I saw everything lying there, it inspired me. The color palette had dark and light and everything in between, creating a harmonious place from which to start. I further exaggerated this by my dark-to-light color choices for the embroidery floss. I created texture by adding buttons, silk ribbon, and beads.

Materials

- 3 antique photographs printed on 8½″ × 11″ sheet of cotton twill PhotoFabric (CTPF) (see Selecting, Scanning, and Printing Photographs on Fabric, page 11)

- Muslin: ½ yard for foundations

- Solids: 1 fat quarter (18″ × 22″) each of 4–6 coordinating fabrics (If you don't want to use solid fabrics, choose fabrics with subtle patterns so the embroidery work will show.)

- Medium brown: ⅓ yard for inner border

- Taupe: ½ yard for outer border

- Paisley: 1 yard for backing and binding

- Cotton batting: 23″ × 42″ (Use the thinnest you can find; I used Warm and Natural.)

- Perle cotton #8 in soft gold, cream, and black

- Embellishments: an assortment of beads, trinkets, keys, embroidery floss, lace, buttons, and silk ribbons—a variety of textures and neutral colors will make the piece look authentically "crazy" when it's finished

Cutting

FABRIC PHOTO

- Fussy cut each photograph into a 5-sided piece. Leave at least ¼″ around the subject in the photograph to allow for the seam allowance when attaching the next pieces of fabric.

Five-sided photograph.

MUSLIN

- Cut 3 squares 10″ × 10″ for the foundations.

SOLIDS

- Cut randomly sized 1½″- to 2½″-wide strips for foundation piecing. Do this quickly by folding the fat quarters twice to create 4 layers of fabric and then cutting many strips in all different widths across the grain. Pile them up and use them for the foundation piecing.

MEDIUM BROWN

- Cut 2 strips 2½″ × 29″ (at least) for the side inner borders.

- Cut 2 strips 2½″ × 14″ for the top and bottom inner borders.

TAUPE

- Cut 2 strips 3½″ × 33″ (at least) for the side outer borders.

- Cut 2 strips 3½″ × 20″ for the top and bottom outer borders.

PAISLEY

- Cut 1 piece 23″ × 42″ for the backing.

- Cut 3 strips 2″ × fabric width for the binding (approximately 124″).

Construction and Embroidery

Press after each step.

1. Pin the 3 photographs to the foundations in the arrangement shown.

2. Use the solid strips to foundation piece each block (see Foundation Piecing, pages 16–19).

3. Draw the designs for your hand embroidery, referring to Design and Drawing (pages 25–27) for guidance.

4. Stitch the embroidery, choosing stitches from Stitching Techniques (pages 28–38). The embroidery for this project is not refined and detailed; rather, it is more primitive looking.

5. Press the blocks.

6. Square each block to 10″ × 10″.

7. Sew the blocks together.

8. Press the seam allowances open to distribute the bulk created by the embroidery.

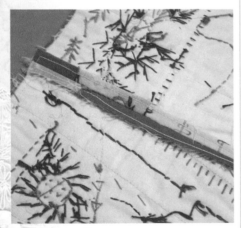

Press seams open.

9. Embroider some pleasing stitches along the 2 seams between the blocks to help unify the finished piece.

10. Age borders, if desired (page 10). Add the 2½″ × 29″ side inner borders; then attach the 2½″ × 14″ top and bottom inner borders.

11. Add the 3½″ × 33″ side outer borders; then attach the 3½″ × 20″ top and bottom outer borders.

Embellishment

Add the embellishments (buttons, keys, etc.).

Try new things. For example, in the first block, buttons are missing in the chain. This may cause a viewer to think and adds to the feeling that the piece is a bit tattered. Everything I've done is to give my brand-new piece a timeless, aged feel.

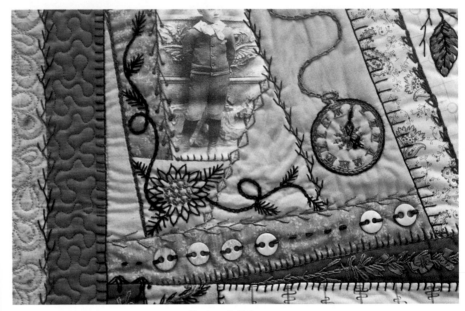

Block embellishments

Finishing

1. Layer the top with the batting and backing and quilt as desired.

2. Add binding. I used a dark paisley fabric for the binding, which helps the entire piece pop. Using the dark binding with the medium and light borders balances the tones in the blocks (see project photo, page 50).

3. Sew ribbons and buttons along the bottom edge.

For the Love of Mother

Made by Brian Haggard, machine quilted by Melissa Taylor | **Finished size:** 30" × 30"

This is the first quilt I ever made. My inspiration was to make a Christmas gift for my mother. The center photo is of my mother, and the one on the bottom is her mother. I'm a third-generation textile artist. My grandma taught me to sew. Many things in this quilt, such as the cobweb, bird, and clover motifs, were inspired by early 1860s crazy quilts. In this quilt, I created vignettes with felt appliqué. No antique or vintage pieces were used to create this look.

Materials

- 3–5 antique photographs printed on 8½″ × 11″ sheet(s) of cotton twill PhotoFabric (CTPF) (see Selecting, Scanning, and Printing Photographs on Fabric, page 11)

- Muslin: ⅔ yard for foundation

- Cream to sepia: 1 fat quarter each of 4 solid or low-contrast cotton fabrics for foundation piecing

- Brown: ⅝ yard for border

- Backing: 1 yard coordinating fabric

- Binding: ⅓ yard coordinating fabric

- Cotton batting: 34″ × 34″ (Use the thinnest you can find; I used Warm and Natural.)

- Cream felt: 1 craft sheet

- Perle cotton #8 in soft gold and cream

- #7 silk ribbon in cream

- Assorted buttons: plastic leaf, mother-of-pearl, nylon scrapbooking buttons, patterned mother-of-pearl

- Lace appliqués (I used white bridal appliqués. A touch of cream spray paint toned them down and made them look vintage.)

- Premade beaded appliqués (Rummage through things on sale tables. These were also wedding white, so I spray painted them to age them.)

Cutting

Honestly, I don't measure this stuff. I just lay out my fabric and cut it with a rotary cutter; wherever it lands, it lands. For me, this makes it more organic and *fun*!

FABRIC PHOTOS

- Crop the photographs as you see fit. Cut a 5-sided photo for the center of the quilt, so that the foundation piecing will be random like a crazy quilt.

MUSLIN

- Cut 1 square 21½″ × 21½″ for the foundation.

BROWN

- Cut 4 strips 4¾″ × fabric width for the border. Trim 2 strips to 4¾″ × 21½″ for the top and bottom borders. Trim 2 strips to 4¾″ × 30″ for the side borders.

CREAM TO SEPIA

- Randomly cut strips 4″–6″ wide for the foundation piecing.

BACKING

- Cut 1 square 34″ × 34″.

BINDING

- Cut 4 strips 2″ × fabric width.

Construction

Press after each step. Use a ¼″ seam allowance.

It doesn't matter whether you sew the fabric strips clockwise or counter-clockwise. However, whichever way you start, you must continue!

1. Pin the center photo (the one with 5 sides) to the foundation at an angle. This will look odd when you start, but it will be fine.

2. Piece the other photos into the solid strips.

Photos pieced into strips

3. Use the solid strips to foundation piece the block (see Foundation Piecing, pages 14–19).

Note

Don't make this hard. Use the photos you pieced into strips exactly like any other strip of fabric. Continue to foundation piece around the center until the entire muslin foundation is covered. Remember to press as you go.

4. Press from the back.

5. Square the block to 21½″ × 21½″.

6. Add the 4¾″ × 21½″ brown border strips to the top and bottom. Add the 4¾″ × 30″ brown border strips to the sides.

Embellishment

1. Draw the embroidery designs, referring to the designs throughout the book for ideas and inspiration. Enjoy the process. It doesn't matter where you start. However, the motifs will be focal points, so you may want to work on these first. The stitching on the seams is a secondary design element, so it makes sense to add these stitches last.

Tip

It's easier if you draw and then stitch one area at a time.

2. Cut felt pieces for the motifs. Lay these out in a design that pleases you, including the appliqués, buttons, and other embellishments you gathered for this project.

3. Begin embroidering the piece, sewing the embellishments as you go. Are you feeling free?

Finishing

1. Layer the top with the batting and backing and quilt as desired.

2. Add binding.

Love Letters

Made by Brian Haggard, machine quilted by Melissa Taylor
Finished size: 23" × 36½"

A dear friend of mine inspired this quilt. The photograph is of us dressed in our 1860s costume ball attire. I created the fabrics and then dissected them to make this piece—so much fun! I started with old love letters I found while antiquing. The use of love letters to tell a love story is a great idea to hand down for generations to come. It doesn't always have to be a love interest, though. In this case, it was about a dear friend, Colleen Anderson. I scanned the altered art (old feathers, love letters, pens, and stamps) into my computer and printed it on fabric. Play with this technique to create your own memories.

Materials

Materials are based on starting with a 5" × 7" photo. Adjust the fabric amounts based on the size of photo you want to use.

- Antique photograph printed on 8½" × 11" sheet of cotton twill PhotoFabric (CTPF) (See Selecting, Scanning, and Printing Photographs on Fabric, page 11). Trim photo (5" × 7"), allowing for a ¼" seam allowance on each side.

- Medium brown: ¼ yard solid or low-contrast cotton fabric for sashing

- Postcard (or other image printed on fabric) to fit in area above photo (5" × 3")

- Muslin: ¼ yard for foundation strips

- Computer-generated love letter fabrics printed on 2 sheets 8½" × 11" of CTPF for foundation-pieced strips

- Darker brown: ¼ yard solid or low-contrast cotton fabric for embroidery

- Floral cotton upholstery fabric (54" wide): 1½ yards for border, backing, and binding

- Cotton batting: 27" × 40" (Use the thinnest you can find; I used Warm and Natural.)

- Perle cotton (I used ecru crochet thread, but why should you?)

- Embellishments (By now you know the drill. I love buttons, especially shell buttons. Think about what you love and want to add to your work of art!)

- Wooden thread spool or other circular found objects to use as templates for embroidery

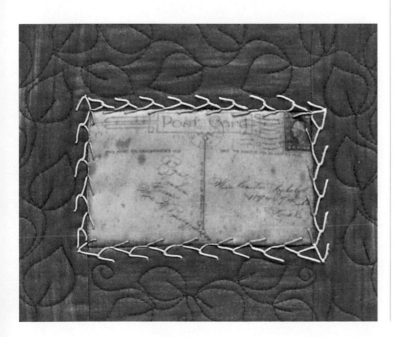

Construction

Press after each step. Use a ¼" seam allowance.

This is going to be easy and fun. Put on some music and start cutting and piecing.

The only foundation piecing I did was with the side strips that I created from the love letters by foundation piecing the dissected fabric to rectangles of muslin.

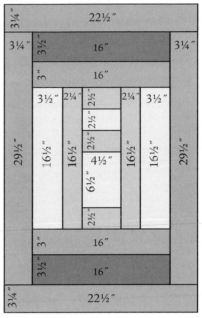

Assembly diagram with finished measurements

The technique in this project uses a cut-as-you-go method, which will work for any size of center photo. The measurements I used to make my quilt are in parentheses in case you prefer more guidance.

1. Cut a medium brown strip the width (3") you prefer × fabric width. Trim into 3 strips (5" × 3") the width of your photo. Add a strip to the top of the photograph; add another strip to the bottom of the photograph. Press. The remaining strip will be added in Step 3.

But then I found the antique postcard. That's right—I didn't have it when I started the piece. But when I found this postcard, I knew it belonged in the quilt. (Are you beginning to see how this works?) I scanned the postcard into my computer, printed it on CTPF, and trimmed it to size.

2. Trim the postcard piece to fit (5" × 3") and add it above the photograph.

I thought another strip of brown fabric would give it nice balance.

3. Add the remaining strip from Step 1 above the postcard.

   The piece was calling for strips of brown on each side to frame the photo and postcard. I obeyed.

4. Cut a medium brown strip the width you prefer (2¾") × fabric width. Trim into 2 strips for the sides (2¾" × 17") and add them.

   The foundation-pieced love letters added a wonderful element.

5. Cut 2 foundation pieces larger than the width and length you need (5" × 18" each) from muslin.

6. Foundation piece the computer-generated fabrics onto the foundations (See Foundation Piecing, pages 16–19). Trim to the length and width you choose (4" × 17").

   At this point, I was planning to add borders of the floral fabric and call it done. But the quilt was not ready for that. I was inspired to elongate the piece to create visual interest at the top and the bottom with the dark brown strips, which also gave me a place to embroider floral motifs. Not knowing what the completed project will be is what keeps me going.

7. Cut a floral strip the width you prefer (3½") × fabric width. Trim 2 strips to size (3½" × 16½") and add them to the top and bottom of the piece

8. Cut a dark brown strip the width you prefer (4") × fabric width. Trim 2 strips to size (4" × 16½") and add them to the top and bottom of the piece.

9. Cut 2 floral strips the width you prefer (3¾") × fabric width. Trim 2 strips to size (3¾" × 30") and add them to the sides.

10. Cut a floral strip the width you prefer (3¾") × fabric width. Trim 2 strips to size (3¾" × 23") and add them to the top and bottom.

Embellishment

Embellish as the piece moves you. I chose simple nylon and pearl buttons to add texture. I then finished with a counter-clockwise featherstitch.

Finishing

1. Cut the backing (27" × 40") at least 3" wider and longer than the finished quilt top. Cut 4 strips 2" wide × fabric width for the binding. (I used 54"-wide fabric and needed just 3 strips.)

2. Layer the top with the batting and backing and quilt as desired. You may want to use a meandering stitch that flows with the overall design.

3. Add binding.

Etta May's Special Day

One of my favorite pictures of my great-grandmother gave me great inspiration for this piece. I already had her graduation diploma. Finding the picture to go with the diploma was the icing on the cake. Crochet thread was always available at my grandmother's, so that's what she used to teach me to embroider. It gives much more detailed stitching than embroidery floss. Later I learned about perle cotton (also used in this piece). It's great to mix the two.

Made by Brian Haggard, machine quilted by Melissa Taylor | **Finished size:** 29″ × 41″

Tip

The diploma was about 16″ × 20″, which is too large for my scanner. I took it to a local copy shop and had it reduced and printed on paper so that I could print it on fabric using my printer.

Think outside the box. You could also use a wonderful hand-made sketch, a marriage license, a birth certificate, or an ancestral charcoal drawing.

I found the perfect faded-looking, gradated background/border fabric in a quilt shop. The fabric fades from a cream to a light brown. This is the only print used in the quilt; the other five fabrics are solids.

I can't help but think that Great-Grandma Etta May Reid would have been proud to see this historical piece made in her honor hanging in my studio. She would be so happy to know she is still part of my quilting adventures. I love you, Grandma.

Tip

You can create the ombré (graduated) effect with a piece of fabric (about 2 yards) and a pot of strong, hot black tea. Start by dipping the fabric within a foot of its top; then pull it up and let it dry. Add the fabric to the pot again, but this time go a quarter of the way down. Repeat until the fabric is graded in color. The already-stained fabric will darken each time you dip it. This is a great project for a summer day. Use a large soup pot that you can keep heating on the stove and take everything out on the porch to dip the fabric. Hang the fabric on a clothesline and let it dry.

Materials

Materials are based on starting with an approximately 7″ × 9½″ photo and a 10″ × 8″ diploma. Adjust the fabric amounts based on the size of the photo or document you want to use.

- Photographs or documents printed on 8½″ × 11″ sheets of cotton twill PhotoFabric (CTPF) (see Selecting, Scanning, and Printing Photographs on Fabric, page 11)

- Print: 1⅓ yards for borders and binding

- Solid cotton: ⅛ yard each of 5 solids

- Backing: 33″ × 45″

- Cotton batting: 33″ × 45″ (Use the thinnest you can find; I used Warm and Natural.)

- Crochet thread, fine weight in cream: 1 skein

- Perle cotton #8 in cream: 1 skein

- Silk ribbon #7 in cream: 1 skein

- Felt, cream: 1 craft sheet

- Buttons

- Appliqués painted with cream aerosol spray paint for timeless aging

Cutting

The size really doesn't matter. I don't measure anything, and you don't have to either! Seriously, what you cut will depend on the number and size of the document(s) and photograph(s) you want to use.

Construction

I can't give you measurements because your pictures and documents will be a different size from mine. Press after each step.

1. I started with the diploma and added borders to the photograph to make it the same width as the diploma.

   The borders can be whatever width you want. (I cut my borders about 3½″, 3″, and 4½″ wide.) I have found that a medium, a smaller, and a larger border make a nice gradation and frame the stitching effectively. Don't sweat it! Just make it work.

2. Cut and add the ombré print top and bottom inner borders.

3. Cut and add the ombré print side inner borders.

4. Foundation piece the side borders crazy-quilt style on long strips of muslin (see Foundation Piecing, pages 16–19).

Tip

Cut the foundation strips for the side borders at least 1″ wider and 4″ longer than you think you will need. This gives some wiggle room; you can always cut off the excess. To keep the random feel, make sure you're foundation piecing at various angles and not in a straight line.

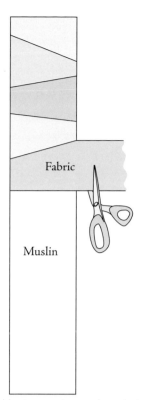

Add strips at various angles and trim.

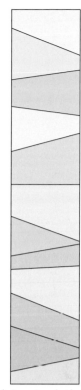

Foundation-pieced side borders

5. Trim the foundation-pieced side borders to the desired size and stitch them to the sides.

6. For the top and bottom foundation-pieced borders, cut a piece of muslin more than twice as wide as the width you want the borders to be and a little longer than the length you want.

7. Starting with a 5-sided piece at the center, add fabric strips that spiral out until the muslin is completely covered. Cut it in half with a rotary cutter and trim to size to make the top and bottom borders.

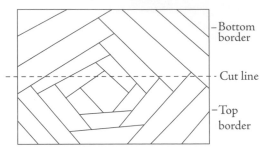

– Bottom border

– Cut line

– Top border

Foundation-pieced block for border

8. Turn the borders around so they look like they were pieced separately. Sew them to the top and bottom of the quilt. This is a quick, easy way to make pieced borders that look random, yet balanced.

9. Cut and add the ombré print side outer borders.

10. Cut and add the ombré print top and bottom outer borders.

Embellishment

Start with a pencil sketch, referring to the designs throughout this book for inspiration.

Finishing

1. Layer the top with the batting and backing and quilt as desired.

2. Add binding.

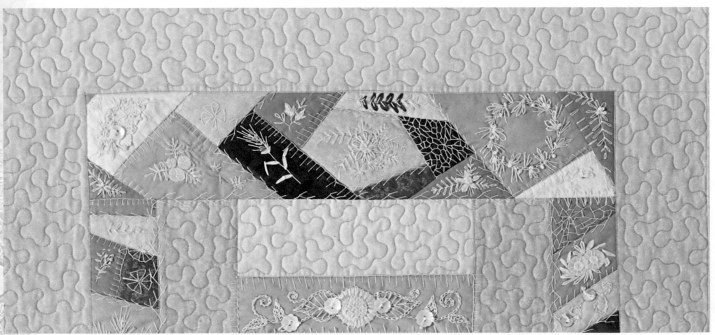

Foundation-pieced border

Button, Button, Who's Got the Button?

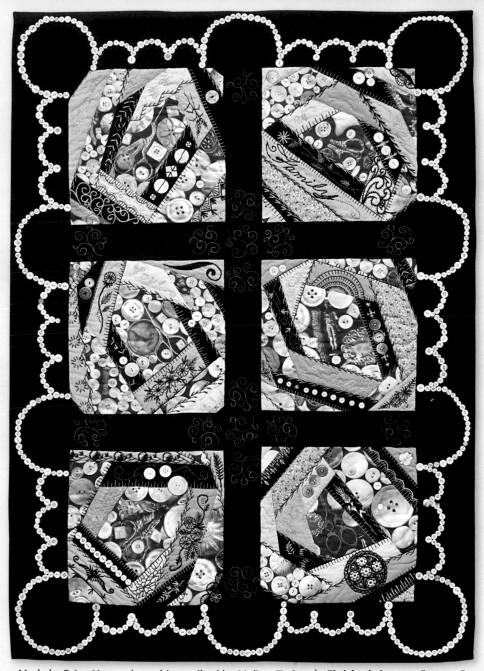

Made by Brian Haggard, machine quilted by Melissa Taylor | **Finished size:** 35½″ × 50½″

*M*y love of buttons and sewing implements inspired this quilt. One day, while going through my collection, I got the idea of placing buttons face down on my scanner in different random patterns and scanning them. I could create my own fabric! Some of my favorite sewing implements were used as the focal point of each block. All the printed fabric used in this quilt was made on the computer. The objects were sized up and down to make them look unique and different (see Manipulating Photographs, page 12). The featured scissors, pins, buttons, and needle cases are things I would love to have found in my grandmother's haberdashery.

Note

This wonderful sewing bird clamp, loaned to me by my good friend Johneva, would have been used in my great-grandmother's haberdashery in the mid 1880s instead of an embroidery hoop. This elegant Victorian implement would have held the fabric in its beak to help the seamstress keep her fabric taut. There are many variations of these clamps that are sought after.

Sewing bird from the collection of Johneva Campbell.
Photo by Brian Haggard

Materials

- 8 computer-generated fabrics printed on 8½″ × 11″ sheets of cotton twill PhotoFabric (CTPF) (see Selecting, Scanning, and Printing Photographs on Fabric, page 11): 6 for focal points of blocks and 2 for foundation piecing

- Muslin: 1 yard for foundation piecing

- Solid neutrals: 3 fabrics (remnants or scraps) for foundation piecing

- Black: 1½ yards for foundation piecing, sashing, borders, and binding

- Backing: 39″ × 54″

- Cotton batting: 39″ × 54″ (Use the thinnest you can find; I used Warm and Natural.)

- Perle cotton #8 in cream, black, and variegated: 1 skein each

- Favorite things lying around the house to scan and manipulate using photo-editing software to create your new piece of art (e.g., buttons, jewelry, Grandma's wedding ring, brooches, lace hankies, scissors, pins . . . the list goes on and on)

- Dessert plate and juice glass for tracing circles

- Lots of buttons! (I used various sizes of vintage pearl shirt buttons, both 2- and 4-hole.)

Cutting

FABRIC PHOTOS

- Fussy cut 6 printed fabric photos into 5-sided shapes.

Tips

- Don't be afraid to cut through an image. Sometimes it makes the photo more visually interesting.

- Once you fussy cut the center photos for the quilt blocks, the excess printed fabric can be used for foundation piecing so nothing is wasted. Cut these extras into random strips 2″–3″ wide to go around the center blocks.

- Cut the remaining 2 printed fabric sheets into strips 2″–3″ wide along the 11″ side.

Tip

Cut the wider strips from the large prints and cut narrow strips from the small prints.

MUSLIN

- Cut 6 squares 12½″ × 12½″ for the block foundations.

SOLID NEUTRAL FABRICS

- Cut random strips 1½″–3″ wide strips so you have a variety of sizes for foundation piecing.

BLACK

- Cut 1 or 2 strips 1″–2″ wide for the foundation piecing.

- Cut 3 strips 3½″ × 12½″ and 2 strips 3½″ × 27½″ for the sashing.

- Cut 2 strips 4½″ × 27½″ for the top and bottom borders.

- Cut 3 strips 4½″ × fabric width. Piece the strips together end to end and trim to get 2 pieces 4½″ × 50½″ for the side borders.

- Cut 5 strips 2″ wide × fabric width for the binding.

Construction

Press after each step.

1. Starting with the 5-sided center photo, stitch the strips of fabric around it to cover the muslin (see Foundation Piecing, pages 16–19). Avoid using strips of the same print next to each other; use solid fabric to break it up and keep it interesting.

2. Make 6 blocks. Trim each to 12½″ × 12½″.

Embellishment

Embellish the blocks before joining them.

This makes a great project for traveling in the car because the blocks fit nicely in your lap. For a fun touch, I added writing in each block. I wrote and embroidered freehand words, such as *scissors*, *family*, *friends*, and so on.

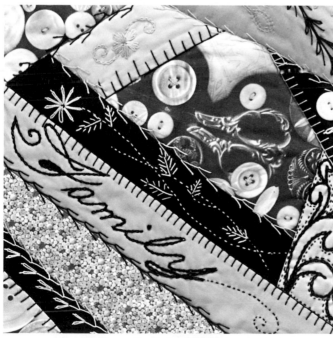
Detail of writing

Some of my blocks were made with a specific design, while others were filled with pattern and texture. Sometimes things fell outside the lines; other times I turned one button upside down. Anywhere I saw an open set of button holes, I stitched through the button image to make it appear sewn on. A discerning viewer may now look at it and ask, "Why?"

Button images are "sewn on."

To make the medallion, I used a juice glass to draw a big circle and a small spool to draw five little, evenly spaced circles inside. I stitched the design using black perle cotton. To finish, I sewed five buttons inside the five little circles.

Detail of stitched medallion

For more embellishment ideas, see Design Inspiration (pages 86–94).

Notice the rows of buttons—I left a button off now and then or put in a very special button to create visual interest. I also used different-sized two- and four-hole buttons to add to the handmade look.

Detail of buttons

Borders

1. Sew a 3½″ × 12½″ sashing strip between 2 foundation-pieced blocks. Repeat to make 3 rows of blocks (see Sashing and Borders, pages 19–20).

2. Sew a 3½″ × 27½″ sashing strip between 2 rows. Repeat to add another 3½″ × 27½″ sashing strip and another block row.

3. Add the 4½″ × 27½″ border strips to the top and bottom of the quilt top and then add the 4½″ × 50½″ strips to the sides.

4. Add the button scallops *before* quilting. I used a white quilter's pencil with a dessert plate and a juice glass to draw lines that I could follow while attaching the buttons.

Finishing

1. Layer the top with the batting and backing and quilt as desired.

2. Add binding.

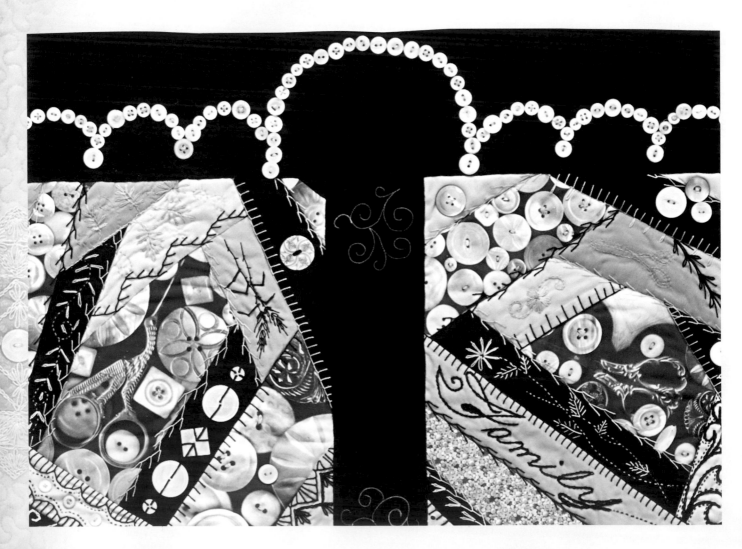

A Family Legacy

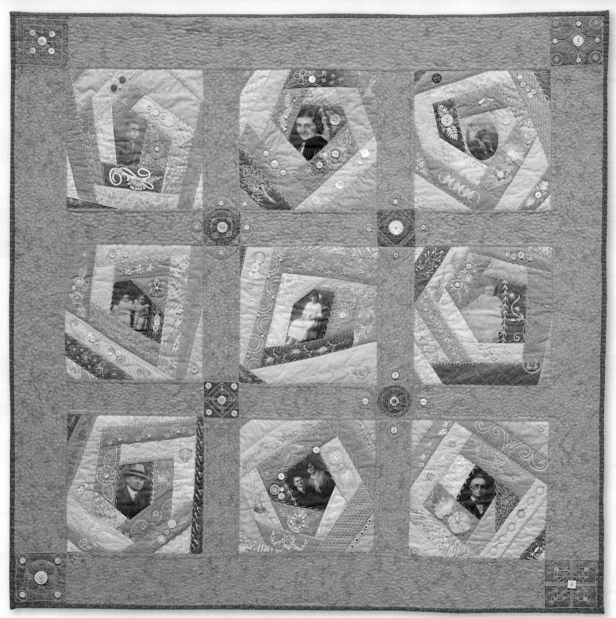

Made by Brian Haggard, machine quilted by Melissa Taylor | **Finished size:** 47½″ × 47½″

This nine-block quilt is a grouping of some favorite photos my grandmothers left me. I used a neutral, monochromatic (tints, tones, and shades of one color) palette. The top middle picture is my grandmother's high school graduation picture, and the middle picture is my great-grandmother's graduation picture. It only seemed right to put my grandfather's graduation photo with them. It was great to use my family history to create this look. While I was making this quilt, my friend, Bev Board, found out what I was doing and donated her mother's collection of buttons, which makes this project extra special because her mother, Peggy Narmore, was a dear friend of mine. Thank you, Bev, for giving me part of your family legacy.

This quilt, which uses my favorite family photographs, is one of my proudest achievements. I'm happy to be able to share it with you. I hope using your family photos and memorabilia will bring you as much happiness.

Materials

- 9 antique photographs printed on 8½″ × 11″ sheets of cotton twill PhotoFabric (CTPF) (see Selecting, Scanning, and Printing Photographs on Fabric, page 11)

- Muslin: 1 yard for block foundations

- Fabrics: ¼ yard each of 7–9 fabrics from cream white to deep beige (I chose mostly solid fabrics and added a couple of fabrics with very light patterns just for background texture.)

- Tan: 1⅛ yards for sashing and borders

- Dark tan: ¼ yard for cornerstones and border corners

- Medium brown: 3¼ yards for backing and binding

- Batting: 51″ × 51″

Cutting

FABRIC PHOTOS

- Fussy cut the fabric photos into 5-sided shapes.

MUSLIN

- Cut 9 squares 11½″ × 11½″ for the block foundations.

FABRICS

- Cut random strips 1½″–2½″ wide × fabric width for the foundation piecing.

TAN

- Cut 12 strips 3½″ × 11½″ for the sashing.

- Cut 4 strips 4½″ × 39½″ for the borders.

DARK TAN

- Cut 4 squares 3½″ × 3½″ for the sashing cornerstones.

- Cut 4 squares 4½″ × 4½″ for the border corners.

MEDIUM BROWN

- Cut 2 pieces 26″ × 51″ for the backing.

- Cut 5 strips 2″ × fabric width for the binding.

Construction

Press after each step. Use a ¼″ seam allowance.

Start with the 5-sided center fabric photo and stitch the strips of fabric around it to cover the muslin (see Foundation Piecing, pages 16–19). Trim to 11½″ × 11½″. Make 9.

Embellishment

Embellish the blocks before sewing them together, so they can travel with you.

My great-grandpa Ernie Reid was a pheasant hunter and fisherman, so I embroidered a pheasant and put a fish button on his block.

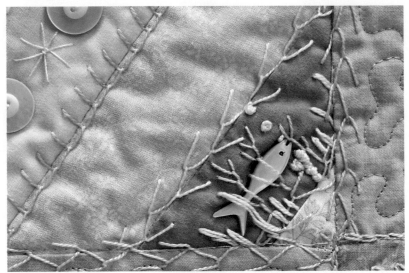

Detail of fish button

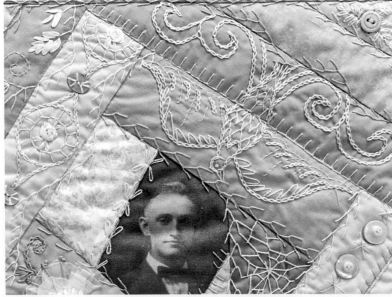

Detail of pheasant embroidery

I love this graduation picture of my grandma Juanita. I embroidered lilacs, because they were her favorite flower, and a seagull from one of her favorite books, *Jonathon Livingston Seagull*.

Detail of Grandma Juanita block

I tried to use one band of texture in each block.

I used organza flowers throughout the quilt. These were made using #9 organza ribbon. One flower is sewn on flat, and the other is folded in half to make it look like a bloom. It's okay to leave some things loose.

Detail of organza flower

Notice how the interior cornerstones are heavily embellished. I drew a square; then I drew triangles inside the square to make a grid to work from. I started with three little leaves, moved to the inside, and did the same thing and liked it, so I repeated this three more times. When I start, I don't know where I'm going. To know would be boring. Instead,

I let the design develop organically as I embroider. I'll tear something out and start over if I don't like where it went. Sometimes it's a happy mistake, and sometimes it's not. Of the four border cornerstone embellishments, two are square and two are curved. They have a similar feel, so the design is balanced. I really enjoyed making these.

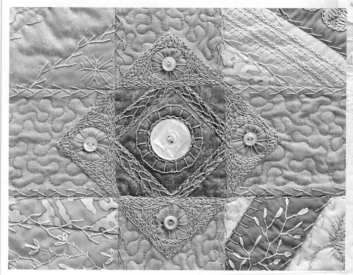

Cornerstone detail

Assembling

1. Assemble the blocks with sashing and cornerstones.

2. Add the borders and corners.

3. Add the final embellishments.

Finishing

1. Sew both 26″ × 51″ backing pieces together along the 51″ edges to create a 51½″ × 51″ backing.

2. Layer the quilt top with the batting and backing and quilt as desired.

3. Add binding.

Silken Tribute

Made by Brian Haggard, machine quilted by Melissa Taylor | **Finished size:** 42″ × 47″

This is not your grandmother's quilt. According to my friend Sandy, this quilt is so beautiful, it can't be described. It's a one-block wonder, created in rich bronze and robin's-egg blue silks and heavily embellished with love for my family. As any quilter knows, fabric is everything. Although I'm usually a cotton-fabric quilter, these silk fabrics spoke to me, and I had that lightbulb mo-

ment. They inspired me, and I knew this was the piece I wanted to make. The big art is in the center of the quilt. A quiet bronze and blue striped border frames it. Finally, a busy foundation-pieced border keeps things interesting. Notice how each little rectangle is its own piece of art.

I hope my silken tribute inspires you to create your own; it is one of my most creative endeavors.

Materials

Materials are based on starting with a 24" × 29" quilt center. Adjust the fabric amounts based on the size of quilt you want.

The technique used to make this project will work for any size of quilt. The measurements I used to make my quilt are in parentheses in case you prefer more guidance.

- Silks: 4¾ yards total; 1 stripe and 3 solids for center and outer border foundation piecing, backing, and binding

- Silk stripe: ¾ yard for inner border (You will need 4 repeats, so purchase extra fabric if necessary for 4 matching border strips.)

- Muslin: 1 yard for foundations

- Silk PhotoFabric (These photos were printed on silk photo-transfer fabric so that they would have the same weight and body as the fabric used in the rest of the quilt.)

- Fusible interfacing (such as Shape-Flex): ½ yard to stabilize silk photos and striped fabric

- Batting: 46" × 51"

Cutting

MUSLIN

- Cut a piece in your chosen size (24" × 29") for the center foundation.

- Cut 1 strip 1" wider than double your chosen finished width (3" × 40½" finished; 7" × 41" cut) for the side borders (see Note below).

- Cut 1 strip 1" wider than double your chosen finished width (3" × 41½" finished, 7" × 42½" cut) for the top and bottom borders.

SILK STRIPE

- Cut 4 strips your chosen width (6½") × fabric width.

Note

A quick way to make the 3"-wide outer borders is to foundation piece an 8"-wide border, trim it to 7" wide, and then cut it in half to make two 3½" wide borders. Once they are sewn onto the finished quilt, they will be 3" wide.

SILKS

- Cut strips 3″–4″ wide × fabric width for the foundation piecing.
- Cut 2 pieces (23¼″ × 51″) for the backing.
- Cut (5) strips 2″ wide × fabric width for binding.

FABRIC PHOTOS

Iron the fusible interfacing onto the back of the photos before cutting.

- Fussy cut the 5-sided center photograph.
- Cut the other photographs straight so you can piece them into the strips.

Construction

Press after each step.

1. Foundation piece the center (see Foundation Piecing, pages 16–19). Use the stripes to your benefit to create horizontal and vertical lines in your design.

2. Trim the center block (24″ × 29″).

3. Add embellishments.

4. Add the 2 striped inner side borders (6½″ × 29″). Add the striped inner top and bottom borders (6½″ × 36″).

5. Foundation piece the outer borders and trim. Make 4 borders total.

6. Add the 2 foundation-pieced outer side borders (3½″ × 41″) to the quilt top. Add the top and bottom outer borders (3½″ × 42″).

7. Embellish the outer borders. I went crazy here!

Finishing

1. Sew 2 backing pieces (23¼″ × 51″) together along the long edges to create the backing (46″ × 51″).

2. Layer the top with the batting and backing and quilt as desired.

3. Add binding.

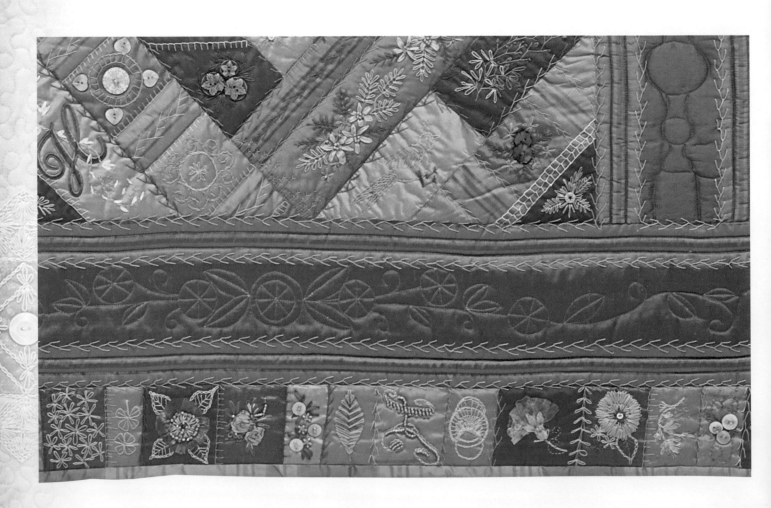

Photo Gallery

A New Twist on Tradition by Brian Haggard, quilted by Melissa Taylor

For all of you traditionalists, here is a way to take one of your sample blocks to make a wonderful gift. Your embroidery transforms the piece into a one-of-a-kind piece of art.

My Traveling Journey by Brian Haggard, quilted by Melissa Taylor

This idea had been brewing for a long time. I collected all my pictures of my European travels and created the sepia-colored border on this quilt to provide instant aging. Old pictures and postcards copied in the center of the quilt were of places I had hoped to venture; I'm happy to say that I've now visited all of them.

B Is for Button by Brian Haggard, quilted by Melissa Taylor

Melissa made me the center initial as a sample. I couldn't let it go to waste, so I started a little one-block project for the car. I added a few borders to make a small wall piece. After it lay on the bench for a few days, it just didn't seem finished, so I decided to enter it in a quilt show. But for that, it had to be larger; so it grew. You can see that it's a quilt within a quilt within a quilt. The ivory felt flowers were originally a garland from an after-Christmas sale. To me, this project defines the notion of letting a project grow organically.

Love, Family, Faith & Hope by Brian Haggard, quilted by Melissa Taylor

Always needing a project in the car, I quickly pieced this wallhanging together the night before a road trip. One picture and a spool of variegated thread paid tribute to my friend Chris's grandmother.

Gert, a Lovely Lady by Brian Haggard

This was a Christmas gift for my friend Chris Opsahl. The photo is of Gert Brown, her mother, at her first Holy Communion. The border fabric is just a snippet of the many yards Chris and I have both used in many, many projects through the years. You can tell we love it!

Gentlemen Callers **by Brian Haggard**

This work means a lot to me because it features the outstanding men from both sides of my family. The young man in the upper-right corner is my dad. My collection of buttons from men's uniforms and work clothes provided the embellishment.

Glory Days by Brian Haggard

This vintage antique purse frame has been given a new life with scraps from the cutting table. The purse was pieced onto foundation fabric and embroidered before being shaped into a new purse to create a fanciful handbag.

Busy Bees by Brian Haggard, quilted by Melissa Taylor

The name reflects the use of appliquéd bees throughout the quilt.
The use of color gives the look of an antique crazy quilt.

Birds of a Feather by Brian Haggard

Inspired by a commercial quilt template, I styled the birds
on this pillow sham so that they gracefully flow over the
seams of the patchwork. Notice how the blue shell buttons
in the center are reversed for added texture. The center H
is a store-bought iron-on initial that I stained with Brian's
Aging Mist.

Pillows by Brian Haggard

I use these pillows as subjects when teaching classes. The pillow to the left is showing a neutral palette but with shades of thread color. The pillow below is showing a monochromatic one color thread to show a neutral palette.

Opal Meets Charlotte by Brian Haggard

This whimsical wallhanging was created from many of my treasures, including some found on my travels. To point out a few, the photo of my grandmother Opal in her heirloom baptism gown, a Frozen Charlotte doll, the Bethlehem pearl button, bone buttons, crocheted pieces, and silk ribbon, as well as antique bobbin lace on the border.

Bathing Beauty by Brian Haggard

This Christmas gift for my friend Colleen Anderson shows what can happen when you repurpose the scraps from shortening some drapes for an interior-decorating job.

Family Gatherings by Brian Haggard, quilted by Melissa Taylor

All four parents of my good friends Chris and Al Opsahl were the driving force behind this quilt. Chris loves black accents, so I gave it a bold black border and black embroidery. The bold contrast of the single-color black thread creates a powerful dimension.

Opal and Ollie: Their Wedding Bliss
by Brian Haggard

The great stash of never-before-seen pictures of my dad's family drove me to create this three-block wallhanging. Always trying something new, I harvested the appliqué in the first block from an antique lace collar—never let anything go to waste. The use of 1930s pajama buttons on the center block created texture and visual interest.

Family Timeless
Pins Needles Sew
Love Joy Hope
Vintage Buttons
Friendship Faith
Forget me Not
Mother Mom
Father Dad
Remembrance
Memories
Birds of a Feather
Journey
Happy Days

About the Author

Brian Haggard is, among other things, a quilt artist living and working in Indianapolis, Indiana. Brian keeps himself busy creating original art in many media, including quilting, embroidery, photography, and altered art. Brian's "day job" is working with his many clients as an interior designer and mural artist. For fun, Brian likes to visit antique shops and quilt stores to look for ideas and embellishments for his work. The fabric, buttons, lace, old photos, keys, clocks, and watches found on these trips are the inspiration for his art and usually appear in his quilts. Brian has always loved old buttons and has recently turned collecting them into a hobby of its own. In fact, he is currently president of the local button club. Brian shares his love of creativity in the classroom and thrills at seeing the joy his students experience as they create beautiful, one-of-a-kind pieces.

Email: mail@brianhaggard.com
Visit my blog at www.brianhaggard.com to keep up with what I'm doing and for more information about my classes and upcoming travels.

Brian's Aging Mist

Brian's Aging Mist comes in a mist bottle. Push down slowly to get a splattered effect or push down quickly to get a fine mist. Depending on the desired look, this tool is very handy for giving a worn look to new, bright items. You can let it dry naturally, or, if you are like I am and have a patience issue, a dry iron is a great tool to keep handy. To heat set, iron until dry. Although this is great to age things, it is not recommended for laundering. The quilts I make are pieces of art and are never laundered. Visit my blog for more information, www.brianhaggard.com.

Some of my favorites:

For beautiful hand-dyed cotton fabrics with a suede finish and great hand in many colors (of course, the neutrals catch my eye) and wonderful gradation packs, see my friends at:

Cherrywood Fabrics
P.O. Box 486
Brainerd, MN 56401
888-298-0967
www.cherrywoodfabrics.com

The Back Door is one of my favorite haunts. Teri Dougherty and Linda Hale run a great quilt shop. I've bought a lot of fabric from them and teach embroidery and quilting classes there.

The Back Door
2503 Fairview Place, Suite W
Greenwood, IN 46142
317-882-2120
www.backdoorquilts.com

I love The Southport Antique Mall. Jane Haganman and Alissa Thompson work hard at making their mall a great destination for antique hounds. When I need inspiration, I take a tour through the mall and always find a little something that sparks a design. A lot of the buttons and embellishments shown on the quilts in this book were found there. If you ever get by to visit, be sure to tell them I sent you.

Southport Antique Mall
2028 East Southport Road
Indianapolis, IN 46227
317 786-8246
www.southportantiquemall.net

Great Titles *from* C&T PUBLISHING

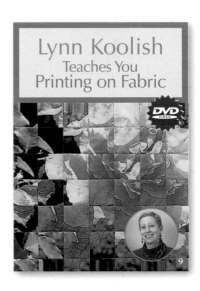

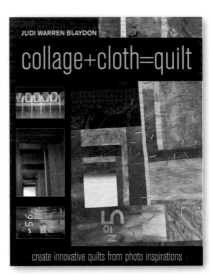

Available at your local retailer or **www.ctpub.com** *or* **800-284-1114**

For a list of other fine books from C&T Publishing, visit our website to view our catalog online.

C&T PUBLISHING, INC.

P.O. Box 1456
Lafayette, CA 94549
800-284-1114

Email: ctinfo@ctpub.com
Website: www.ctpub.com

C&T Publishing's professional photography services are now available to the public. Visit us at www.ctmediaservices.com.

Tips and Techniques can be found at www.ctpub.com > Consumer Resources > Quiltmaking Basics: Tips & Techniques for Quiltmaking & More

For quilting supplies:

COTTON PATCH

1025 Brown Ave.
Lafayette, CA 94549
Store: 925-284-1177
Mail order: 925-283-7883

Email: CottonPa@aol.com
Website: www.quiltusa.com

Note: Fabrics used in the quilts shown may not be currently available, as fabric manufacturers keep most fabrics in print for only a short time.